W9-ASO-706

The Verse Satire

by

JOHN HEATH-STUBBS

OXFORD UNIVERSITY PRESS

1969

Oxford University Press, Ely House, London W. 1
GLASGOW NEW YORK TORONTO MELBOURNE WELLINGTON
CAPE TOWN SALISBURY IBADAN NAIROBI LUSAKA ADDIS ABABA
BOMBAY CALCUTTA MADRAS KARACHI LAHORE DACCA
KUALA LUMPUR SINGAPORE HONG KONG TOKYO

FILMSET AND PRINTED BY ST PAUL'S PRESS LTD, MALTA

Contents

Acknowledgements

The author and publishers gratefully acknowledge permission granted by the following copyright owners to quote from their works:

Penguin Books Ltd, for *New Writing in Europe* by J. Lehmann; Messrs. Faber and Faber for *Introduction to the Selected Poems of Ezra Pound* by T. S. Eliot; Messrs. Faber and Faber and Harcourt, Brace and World for *The Hippopotamus* by T. S. Eliot; The Macmillan Company for *Your Immortal Memory, Burns* by H. MacDiarmid; Jonathan Cape Ltd. and Curtis Brown Ltd. for *The Wayzgoose* by R. Campbell; The Bodley Head for *The Georgiad* by R. Campbell; Curtis Brown Ltd. and Random House Inc., for *Letter to Lord Byron* by W. H. Auden; The Society of Authors and Viking Press Inc. for *The Holy Office* by James Joyce; A. P. Watt and Son and Random House Inc. for *Claudius the God* by R. Graves; Associated Book Publishers Ltd. for *One Way Song* by W. Lewis; Professor Quentin Bell for *Epistle On Wittgenstein* by J. Bell.

I

The Roman Models

In a broad sense, satire is one of the most ancient and universal forms of poetry – if only because rage and scorn are universal human emotions, and mockery and ridicule are universal forms of human expression. Basically, satiric poetry has something of the nature of the primitive ritual curse to which magical effects were attributed. The poets of ancient Ireland were supposed to be able to raise blotches on the faces of those against whom they directed their satirical verses. Another very widespread form of early poetry was what was known among the Provençal troubadours as the *estrif*, and in medieval Scotland as a flyting. This was a contest in the exchange of often only half serious abuse between two poets. Formalized outlets for the aggressive and anti-authoritarian emotions play an important social and psychological role. In primitive societies they were often associated with seasons of permitted licence, especially the harvest and vintage festivals. Both the Greek comic drama and Latin satirical poetry appear to owe their origin to such festivals.

The literary tradition of satirical verse in English derives mainly from Latin models. We therefore begin this book with a brief sketch of the origins and development of classical Latin satire. Latin literature in general leaned heavily on Greek examples, but the word satire (*satura*) was of Latin origin, and the Romans were proud to claim the form as a purely native growth. The Greek equivalent had been iambic poetry (so called because written in the iambic metre, which was regarded as closest in rhythm to prose). But only a few fragments of the work of such Greek iambic poets as **Archilochus** (fl. 648 B.C.) have come down to us, and they did not directly provide models for the Roman writers.

The Latin word *satura* originally meant a miscellany. The derivation accepted by most scholars is from the *satura lanx*. This was a ritual dish containing offerings of first-fruits of various kinds, which formed part of the celebrations of the ancient Roman harvest festival. From this the name was transferred to the scurrilous verses which as we have already said, are frequently associated with such festivals in primitive cultures.

A false etymology, which became widely current in the Renaissance period, connected the word satire with the Greek *saturos*, a satyr. It must be mentioned because it often influenced not only the spelling of the word in English in the sixteenth and seventeenth centuries, but also the conception of the form itself. Since the mythical satyr, half man and half goat, was rough and shaggy, and uninhibited in his behaviour, it was thought proper that literary satire should be the same. This is partly the reason for the extreme roughness of the language, and outspokenness to the point of obscenity, which we find in the satires of such writers as Marston and Donne. This theory was also due to a confusion with the Greek satyr play. The latter, which was performed along with the tragic trilogy, had a chorus of satyrs, and treated a mythical or heroic subject in a more or less light-hearted way. The *Cyclops* of Euripides, which Shelley translated, is the only example which has come down to us complete.

The founder of Roman literary satire was **Lucilius** (148–103 B.C.). His work survives only in fragments. He was a member of Scipio's circle, and altered the traditional form to turn it into a commentary on the politics, literature, and manners of the day. He provided the model for **Horace** (65–8 B.C.), whose influence on the later development of satire has been paramount. Horace's satires are in the form of epistles, addressed to various friends and patrons; their model is the *sermo*, or moral and philosophical essay, employed by the Cynic and Stoic philosophers as a means of instruction. The metre is the Latin hexameter, derived from the Greek, and generally otherwise associated with heroic and narrative poetry. Horace's tone is urbane and conversational. He writes as a detached observer, commenting on the human, social and literary foibles of his day. The following passage is from the translation of the nineteenth century scholar, John Conington (1825–69):

How comes it, say, Maecenas, if you can,
That none will live like a contented man
Where choice or chance directs, but each must praise
The folk who pass through life by other ways?
'Those lucky merchants!' cries the soldier stout,
When years of toil have well-nigh worn him out:
What says the merchant, tossing o'er the brine?
'Yon soldier's lot is happier, sure, than mine:
One short, sharp shock, and presto! all is done:
Death in an instant comes, or victory's won.'
The lawyer lauds the farmer, when a knock
Disturbs his sleep at crowing of the cock:
The farmer, dragged to town on business, swears
That only citizens are free from cares.
I need not run through all: so long the list,
Fabius himself would weary and desist.

The *Ibis* of **Ovid** (43 B.C.–A.D. 18) belongs, as Dryden said, to the underwoods of satire. It is not a discourse covering moral and social matters like the satires of Horace but a piece of pure invective directed against a personal enemy, who had apparently been one of those responsible for Ovid's banishment to the Black Sea coast. This enemy Ovid calls Ibis – possibly because of the unclean and scavenging habits of that Egyptian bird. For this kind of thing there were Greek models, but the poem also partakes of something of the nature of the primitive magical curse. In the space of six hundred and forty-four lines, Ibis is devoted to every sort of misery through life and after death. The following is a specimen, from the translation of Thomas Underdowne (born *c.* 1543?):

> Let the earth deny thee fruit, and stream
> his waters hold from thee;
> Let every wind deny fit blasts
> for thy commodity;
> Let not the sun shine bright on thee,
> nor glistering moon by night,
> And of thy eyes let glimpsing stars
> forsake the wished light;
> Let not the fire grant thee his heat,
> nor air humidity;
> Let neither earth nor yet the sea
> free passage grant to thee:
> That banished and poor thou mayest
> strange houses seek in vain,
> That craving too with trembling voice
> small almes may'st obtain;
> That neither sound of body, nor
> thy mind in perfect plight,
> This night be worse than passed day,
> and next day than this night;
> That thou may'st still be pitiful,
> but pitied of none;
> And that no man nor woman may
> for thy mischances moan.

Although through the medieval and renaissance periods Ovid was probably the most widely read of classical poets, this particular poem does not seem much to have affected English writers, unless traces of its influence may be detected in some passages of dramatic and satiric invective.

The two other principal Roman satirists in verse are **Persius** (A.D.

34–62) and **Juvenal** (A.D. *c.* 60–*c.* 130). Persius is the author of a series of six fairly short satires. His language is extremely difficult, and the obscurity has been rendered even greater by the fact that they were originally written in the form of dialogues between two speakers, which the manuscript text did not indicate clearly. Persius wrote during the reign of Nero, when to speak plainly might have been dangerous. His obscurity, therefore, may partly be intentional. The moral tone of Persius is influenced by the philosophy of the Stoics and Cynics. It should be noted that ancient Cynicism did not imply the irresponsible rejection of all values with which in modern colloquial parlance the word has come to be associated. The Cynics taught that man should live according to nature. His real needs were few and his moral duties simple and obvious. Hence they scoffed at the luxury of the rich, and at the intellectual pretensions of more metaphysically-minded philosophers. In his second satire Persius attacks those who try to bribe the gods with offerings, in order to secure their own material prosperity. As a contrast, he ends with a picture of the man who worships in true humility and sincerity of heart (the translation is that of William Gifford):

One whom in Secret Service she cou'd trust;
Why bring your passions to the Immortals' shrine
And judge, from what this carnal sense delights,
Of what is pleasing in their purer sights?
The flesh Calabrian wool with purple soils,
And mingles cassia with our native oils,
Tears from the rocky couch its pearly store,
And strains the metal from the glowing ore.
The flesh indeed is vicious; yet it tends
To gladden life perhaps, and boasts its ends.
But ye, ye priests (for sure ye can) unfold:
In heavenly things what boots this pomp of gold?
No more, indeed, than dolls to Venus paid
(The toys of childhood) by a riper maid.
No! let me bring the gods what that blear-eyed
Descendant of great Messala can't provide
Out of his lordly salver – bring a mind
Where legal and where moral sense are joined
With the Sure Essence; holy thoughts that dwell
In the soul's most retired and secret cell;
A bosom steeped in honour's noblest grain,
Deep-dyed. With these let me approach the fane,
And Heaven will hear the humble prayer I make,
Though all my offering be a barley cake.

Juvenal's tone is very different from that of Horace. There is nothing light or urbane about it. He is a writer of great power, with a blistering and savage wit. Underlying this is a real moral indignation at the corruptions of Roman society as he had known them under the emperor Domitian. He writes of the miserable life of an impoverished hanger-on of great men, which he himself had experienced, and among his principal targets are sexual licence and perversion, and the moral hypocrisy of professional philosophers. We quote from Dryden's translation of the Sixth Satire, which is devoted to a denunciation of the vices of women. In this passage Juvenal gives as an example the notorious behaviour of Messalina, the wife of Claudius:

> The good old Sluggard but began to snore,
> When from his side up rose th'Imperial Whore:
> She who preferr'd the Pleasures of the Night
> To Pomps, that are but impotent delight;
> Strode from the Palace, with an eager pace,
> To cope with a more Masculine Embrace;
> Muffled she march'd, like Juno in a Clowd,
> Of all her Train but one poor Wretch allow'd,
> One whom in Secret Service she cou'd trust;
> The Rival and Companion of her Lust.
> To the known Brothel-house she takes her way;
> And for a nasty Room gives double pay;
> That Room in which the rankest Harlot lay.
> Prepar'd for fight, expectingly she lies,
> With heaving Breasts, and with desiring Eyes:
> Still as one drops, another takes his place,
> And baffled still succeeds to like disgrace.
> At length, when friendly darkness is expir'd,
> And every Strumpet from her Cell retir'd,
> She lags behind, and lingring at the Gate,
> With a repining Sigh, submits to Fate:
> All Filth without, and all a Fire within,
> Tir'd with the Toyl, unsated with the Sin,
> Old *Caesar's* Bed the modest Matron seeks;
> The steam of Lamps still hanging on her Cheeks,
> In Ropy Smut: thus foul, and thus bedight,
> She brings him back the Product of the Night.

Besides the tradition of Latin verse satire we have dealt with above there was also the so-called Menippean or Varronian satire. This form was originated by the Greek Cynic philosopher **Menippus** (first half of third century B.C.). It consisted of a burlesque prose narrative, interlarded with passages of verse. It incorporated quotations from Homer and the tragic poets, and parodies of them, and is thus, in a sense, a forerunner of the later mock heroic poem. Its principal Latin exponent was **Varro** (116–27 B.C.), but only fragments of his work survive. The *Satyricon* of **Petronius Arbiter** (died *c.* A.D. 65) also belongs to this class. A considerable part of this highly entertaining work has come down to us. It is really in the nature of a realistic picaresque novel.

Another example of Varronian satire is the *Apocolocyntosis* of the philosopher and dramatist **Seneca** (d. A.D. 65). It survives in a nearly complete form. It is a satire on the apotheosis, or official deification after his death, of the Emperor Claudius. The title is translated by Mr. Robert Graves as 'The Pumpkinification', and is probably a joke on the Stoic idea of God as a perfect sphere. Seneca was tutor to Claudius' successor, Nero, though he subsequently (like Petronius) fell out of favour with him and was forced to commit suicide. The work mocks at the person of the deceased Emperor, who was pedantic, lame, uncouth and a stammerer. His real merits as a rather conscientious administrator are given no credit, and there is some very fulsome flattery of the young Nero:

He is sweet Lucifer who puts to flight
The lesser stars; or Hesperus is he
Who swims up clear when back the stars return;
Nay, rather he's the Sun himself, what time
The blushing Goddess of the Dawn leads in
The earliest light of day, dispersed the shades –
The Sun himself with shining countenance
Who pores upon the world, and from the gates
Of his dark prison whirls his chariot out.
A very Sun is NERO and all Rome
Shall look on NERO with bedazzled eyes,
His face a-shine with regal majesty
And lovelocks rippling on his shapely neck.

The translation is that of Robert Graves, printed as an appendix to his historical novel *Claudius The God*. The narrative tells how Claudius journeys to Olympus:

First, a message came to Jove that someone was at the gate, a tallish man, with white hair; he seemed to be uttering some threat or other because he kept on shaking his head; and when he walked he dragged his right foot. He had been asked his nationality and had answered in a confused nervous manner, and his language could not be identified. It was not Greek or Latin or any other known speech.

Jove told Hercules, who had once travelled over the whole earth and so might be expected to know all nations in it, to go and find out where the stranger came from. Hercules went, and though he had never been daunted by all the monsters in the world, he really got quite a shock at the sight of this new sort of creature with its curious mode of progression and its raucous inarticulate voice, which was like that of no known terrestrial animal but suggested some strange beast of the sea. Hercules thought that his Thirteenth Labour was upon him. However, he looked more closely and decided that it was some kind of a man.

Claudius' claim to deification is debated by the gods in council. It is strongly opposed by his imperial predecessor Augustus, now himself deified, especially on the grounds of Claudius' murder of his relations, Augustus' descendants. He is condemned to the infernal regions where his punishment is eternally to rattle a dice box with no bottom to it. In his life Claudius had been notorious for his love of dice playing. The *Apocolocyntosis*, amusing in itself, is of interest to readers of English literature as providing the model for Byron's *The Vision of Judgment*.

2

Tudor Satire

The Roman satirists continued to be read throughout the Middle Ages. Juvenal in particular was treated as a standard school text. His outspoken denunciations of sexual vice were acceptable to the monastic spirit, in spite of or even because of their frankness. The Sixth Satire especially seems to have inspired a whole school of anti-feminist writing. The denigration of women was a persistent, if to us a not very attractive, feature of medieval culture – the reverse of the medal of the idealization of women represented by the courtly love poetry of the troubadours, and the cult of the Blessed Virgin. In medieval vernacular poetry the satirical spirit is widespread. Especially in the later Middle Ages it is frequently directed against the corruptions of the Church, notably the monastic orders, the friars, and the sale of indulgences. This satire often takes an allegorical form, and a notable vehicle of it is the animal fable, as in the 'beast epic' of *Reynard the Fox*. The *Roman de la Rose*, in its second part by **Jean de Meung** (A.D. 1250?–1305?) is also full of outspoken satire. This poem was an important influence on the poetry of the fourteenth century and especially on Chaucer. **Geoffrey Chaucer** (1345(6)?–1400) is indeed a major satirical poet in his own right. This can be illustrated by such parts of the *Canterbury Tales* as *The Pardoner's Prologue* and *The Wife Of Bath's Prologue*. But his art as a satirist is completely fused with that of the narrative poet. The other great English poet of the fourteenth century, **William Langland** (1330?–1400?) also has much of the satirical temper. But *Piers Plowman* transcends the satirical *genre*. It may be regarded as an allegorical epic in which the whole society of the time, and the whole destiny of man, are viewed within a theological context. It is thus the nearest English analogue to Dante's *Divine Comedy*. It requires, however, notice here because it seems to have been regarded by readers of the sixteenth century as primarily a satire, and thus, as we shall see, played a part in the development of satire as a separate *genre*. It may be noted that Dante's poem appears to have been looked at in much the same way by Italian critics of the Renaissance period.

It is to the awakening humanism of the early sixteenth century that we owe the conception of satire as a distinct and separate form. It is thus with two poets of the reign of Henry VIII that we can most usefully begin our survey of English satirical poetry. *The Ship of Fools* by **Alexander Barclay** (1475?–1552) is a translation of the *Narrenschiff* of the German writer **Sebastian Brandt** (1457–1521). This latter work had a European reputation and was translated into many other languages besides English. In it the author imagines a ship lying in harbour with all the different kinds of fools on board. Their characteristic vices are then categorized, in the spirit of medieval sermon literature. There is no action, and little particularity of character drawing in the poem, and nothing is made of the overall scheme of the ship itself. Barclay follows his original quite freely, as his 'Argument' prefixed to the work makes clear:

Here after foloweth the Boke named the Shyp of Foles of the world: translated out of Laten, French and Doche into Englysse in the Colege of saynt Mary Otery By me Alexander Barclay to the felicite and moste holsom instruccion of mankynde.

. . . .

But concernynge the translation of this Boke: I exhort ye reders to take no displesour for it is nat translated worde by worde acordinge to ye verses of my actour. For I haue but only drawen into our moder tunge, in rude langage the sentences of the verses as nere as the parcyte of my wyt wyl suffer me, some tyme addynge, sometyme detractinge and takinge away such thinges as semeth me necessary and superflue.

. . . .

I haue in many places ouerpassed dyuers poetical digressions and obscurenes of Fables and have concluded my worke in rude langage as shal apere in my translacion.

Barclay begins by treating of 'inprofytable bokes'. Here he gently pokes fun at himself:

I am the firste fole of all the hole nauy
To kepe the pompe, the helme and eke the sayle
For this is my mynde, this one pleasoure haue I
Of bokes to haue grete plenty and aparayle
I take no wysdome by them: nor yet auayle
Nor them preceyue nat: And then I them despyse
Thus am I a foole and all that sewe that guyse

That in this shyp the chefe place I gouerne
By this wyde see with folys wanderynge
The cause is playne, and easy to dyscerne
Styll am I besy bokes assemblynge
For to haue plenty it is a plesaunt thynge
In my conceyt and to haue them ay in honde
But what they mene do I nat vnderstonde

But yet I haue them in great reuerence
And honoure sauynge them from fylth and ordure
By often brusshynge, and moche dylygence
Full goodly bounde in pleasaunt couerture
Of domas, satyn, or els of veluet pure
I kepe them sure ferynge lyst they sholde be lost
For in them is the connynge wherin I me bost.

As we have said, *The Ship of Fools* for the most part describes vices and follies in very general moralizing terms. There are, however, occasionally more graphic touches, as in the following passage 'Of newe fassions and disgised garmentes'. The extravagances of contemporary fashion have, of course, been a target for moralists in every age.

Yet fynde I another sort almoste as bad as thay.
As yonge Jentylmen descended of worthy Auncetry.
Whiche go ful wantonly in dissolute aray.
Counterfayt, disgised, and moche vnmannerly
Blasinge and garded: to lowe or else to hye.
And wyde without mesure: theyr stuffe to wast thus gothe
But other some they suffer to dye for lacke of clothe

Some theyr neckes charged with colers, and chaynes
As gold withtthes: theyr fyngers ful of rynges:
Theyr neckes naked: almoste vnto the raynes
Theyr sleues blasinge lyke to a Cranys wynges
Thus by this deuysinge suche counterfayted thinges
They dysfourme that figure that god hymselfe hath made
On pryde and abusion thus ar theyr myndes layde.

Barclay's contemporary, **John Skelton** (1460?–1529), is altogether a livelier and more original poet. Although he possessed a delicate lyrical gift, which he displayed occasionally in both amorous and religious poetry, the major part of his work is satirical. He is one of the great masters of invective, often violent and coarse, but tremendously effective. The verse of the fifteenth and early sixteenth centuries suffered from a weakness of rhythm. This was apparently due to uncertainty as to the pronunciation of the final *-e*. Skelton's peculiar genius enabled him actually to take advantage of this situation, by making his own the type of verse which is hence known as Skeltonic. This is a short line, usually varying between two or three stresses, and with an indefinite number of syllables. These lines rhyme together in couplets, or for as long as the poet can find rhymes. For Skelton has an extravagant feeling for words for their own sake, which is akin to that of his contemporary Rabelais, or of James Joyce. He also resembles both these writers in the delight he shows in displaying his out of the way learning, and in his macaronic habit of interpolating phrases and passages in Latin, Greek and other languages in his work.

The Bouge of Court is one of Skelton's poems written not in Skeltonics but in the rhyme-royal stanza inherited from Chaucer. The scheme of the poem seems to owe something to the *Narrenschiff*. It is in the medieval form of an allegorical vision. The narrator, called Dede, sees a rich merchant ship 'The Bouge of Court' (the rewards of court) whose mistress is the Lady Fortune. But when he embarks upon it, he encounters a crew of thoroughly disreputable characters – Favell, Suspect, Harvy Hafter, Disdain, Riot, Dissimulation and Deceit. These characters are more than mere allegorical abstractions. They prefigure the personages of Jonsonian comedy. Here is Riot:

'Welcome', quod Riot, 'I make God avow.

'And, sir, in faith why com'st not us among
   To make thee merry, as other fellows done?
Thou must swear and stare, man, all day long,
   And wake all night, and sleep till it be noon;
   Thou mayest not study, or muse on the moon;
This world is nothing but eat, drink, and sleep,
And thus with us good company to keep.

'Pluck up thine heart upon a merry pin,
   And let us laugh a pluck or twain at nale:
What the devil, man, mirth is here within!
   What, lo man, see here of dice a bale!
   A birdling-cast for that is in thy male!
Now have at all that lieth upon the board!
Fie on these dice, they be not worth a turd!

'Have at the hazard, or at the dozen brown,
   Or else I pass a penny to a pound!
Now, would to God, thou woulde lay money down!
   Lord, how that I would cast it full round!
Ay, in my pouch a buckle I have found,
The arms of Calais, I have no coin nor cross!
I am not happy, I run aye on the loss.

'Now run must I to the stewes side
   To weet if Malkin, my lemman, have got ought:

I let her to hire, that men may on her ride,
Her armes easy far and near is sought:
By Goddes side, since I her hither brought
She hath got me more money with her tail
Than hath some ship that into Bordeaux sail.'

The most characteristic of Skelton's satires, however, are *Speak, Parrot*, *Colin Clout*, and *Why Come Ye Not to Court?* They deal with the corruptions of the court, of the Church, and with Skelton's deep-seated personal animosity against Cardinal Wolsey. *Speak, Parrot* is a difficult, but extraordinarily original and effective poem. The parrot, the plaything of court ladies, chatters away in the several languages it knows, apparently at random, but continually speaking out with the most pointed and dangerous criticism of what it observes. The bird itself is vividly realized:

My name is Parrot, a bird of Paradise,
By nature devised of a wondrous kind,
Daintily dieted with divers delicate spice
Till Euphrates, that flood, driveth me into Ind;
Where men of that country by fortune me find
And send me to greate ladyes of estate:
Then Parrot must have an almond or a date.

. . . .

With my beke bent, my little wanton eye,
My feathers fresh as is the emerald green,
About my neck a circulet like the rich ruby,
My little legges, my feet both feat and clean,
I am a minion to wait upon a queen:
'My proper Parrot, my little pretty fool!'
With ladies I learn, and go with them to school.

'Ha! Ha! Ha! Parrot, ye can laugh prettily!'
Parrot hath not dined all this long day.
Like your puss-cat, Parrot can mew and cry!
In Latin, in Hebrew, Arabic and Chaldy,
In Greeke tongue Parrot can both speak and say
As Persius, that poet, doth report of me,
Quis expedivit psittaco suum 'chaire'?

In the following passage Skelton seems to be glancing at Wolsey, under the title of Zadok the priest:

Pass forth, Parrot, towards some passenger
Require him to convey you over the salte foam;

Addressing yourself, like a sad messenger,
  To our sullen seignor Sadok, desire him to come home,
  Making his pilgrimage by *Nostre Dame de Crome*:
For Jericho and Jersey shall meet together as soon
As he to exploit the man out of the moon.

With porpoise and grampus he may feed him fat,
  Though he pamper not his paunche with the Great Seal:
We have longed and looked long time for that,
  Which causeth poor suitors have many a hungry meal:
  As president and regent he ruleth every deal.
Now pass forth, good Parrot, our Lord be your steed,
In this your journey to prosper and speed!

In a later passage Skelton is much more outspoken:

Franticness doth rule and all thing command;
  Wilfulness and brainless now rule all the ray;
  Against frantic frenzy there dare no man say nay;
For franticness and wilfulness, and brainless ensemble,
The neb of a lion they make to trete and tremble;

To jumble, to stumble, to tumble down like fooles,
  To lour, to droop, to kneel, to stoop, and to play couch quail,
To fish afore the net and to draw pooles;
  He maketh them to bear baubles, and to bear a low sail;
  He carrieth a king in his sleeve, if all the world fail;
He faceth out at a flush with 'Shew, take all!'
Of Pope Julius' cards he is chief cardinall.

He triumpeth, he trumpeth, he turneth all up and down,
  With 'Skirgalliard, proud palliard, vauntperler, ye prate!'
His wolf's head, wan, blue as lead, gapeth over the crown:
  It is to fear lest he would wear the garland on Lio pate;
  Paregal with all princes far passing his estate:
For of our regent the regiment he hath, *ex qua vi,*
Patet per versus, quod *ex vi bolte harvi,*

Colin Clout, written in Skeltonics, is more popular in tone. In this poem Skelton assumes the *persona* of a wandering vagabond, who goes among the people, witnessing the corrupt state of society and especially the Church:

And if ye stand in doubt
Who brought this rhyme about,
My name is Colin Clout.

I purpose to shake out
All my conning bag,
Like a clerkly hag.
For though my rhyme be ragged,
Tattered and jagged,
Rudely rain-beaten,
Rusty and moth-eaten,
If ye take well therewith,
It hath in it some pith.

For, as far as I can see,
It is wrong with each degree:
For the temporality
Accuseth the spirituality;
The spiritual again
Doth grudge and complain
Upon the temporal men:
Thus each of other blother
The one against the other:
Alas, they make me shudder!
For in hugger-mugger
The Church is put in fault;
The prelates ben so haut,
They say, and look so high,
As though they woulde fly
Above the starry sky.

This poem perhaps shows the influence of the tradition of Langland. It should be noted that in spite of his radical criticisms of the ecclesiastical hierarchy, and the fact that, as a priest he got into serious trouble with the authorities for marrying, Skelton had no sympathy with the Protestant doctrines which were already beginning to infiltrate among the people:

For it maketh me sad
How that the people are glad
The Church to deprave;
And some there are that rave,
Presuming on their wit,
When there is never a whit
To maintain arguments
Against the sacraments.

Some make epilogation
Of high predestination;

And of recidivation
They make interpretation
Of an awkward fashion;
And of the prescience
Of divine essence;
And what hypostasis
Of Christ's manhood is.
Such logic men will chop,
And in their fury hop,
When the good ale sop
Doth dance in their foretop!
Both women and men,
Such ye may well know and ken,
That against priesthoad
Their malice spread abroad,
Railing heinously
And disdainously
Of priestly dignities,
And their malignities.

And some have a smack
Of Luther's sack,
And a burning spark
Of Luther's wark,
And are somewhat suspect
In Luther's sect;
And some of them bark,
Clatter and carp
Of that heresiarch
Called Wicliffista,
The devilish dogmatista;
And some be Hussians,
And some be Arians,
And some be Pelagians,
And make much variance
Between the clergy
And the temporalty,
How the Church hath too mickle,
And they have too little.

Why Come Ye Not to Court? is Skelton's most daring and outspoken satire. In *Speak, Parrot* he had attacked Wolsey covertly and obliquely, but here he devotes an entire work to a diatribe against the Cardinal. Wolsey is held up to scorn for his low origins, his luxury and alleged vices, but above all for his overweening pride. He sets himself up as the equal or almost the superior of the king. This from the medieval and Renaissance point of view is satanic – the great blasphemy against the overriding principle of degree:

> *Why come ye not to court?*
> To which court?
> To the king's court,
> Or to Hampton Court?
> *Nay, to the kinge's court!*
> The kinges court
> Should have the excellence,
> But Hampton Court
> Hath the preeminence,
> And Yorkes Place,
> With my Lordes Grace!
> To whose magnificence
> Is all the confluence,
> Suits and supplications,
> Embassades of all nations.
> Straw for Law Canon,
> Or for the Law Common,
> Or for the Law Civil!
> It shall be as he will.

Wolsey was Archbishop of York. Hampton Court was of course built by him as his own palace, though he was subsequently compelled to make a gift of it to Henry VIII. The poem characteristically builds up to a scarifying and grotesque climax:

> Such a prelate, I trow,
> Were worthy to row
> Through the straits of Marock
> To the jibbet of Baldock!
> He would dry up the streams
> Of nine kings' reams,
> All rivers and wells,
> All waters that swells!
> For with us he so mells,
> That within England dwells,
> I would he were somewhere else:
> For else by and by
> He will drink us so dry,
> And suck us so nigh,

That men shall scantly
Have penny or halfpenny.
God save his noble Grace,
And grant him a place
Endless to dwell
With the Devil of hell!
For, an he were there,
We need never fear
Of the fiendes blake:
For I undertake
He would so brag and crake
That he would then make
The devils to quake,
To shudder and to shake,
Like a fire-drake,
And with a coal-rake
Bruise them on the brake,
And bind them to a stake,
And set hell on fire
At his owne desire.
He is such a grim sire,
He is such a potestolate,
And such a potestate,
That he would break the brains
Of Lucifer in his chains,
And rule them each one
In Lucifer's throne.

Both Barclay and Skelton, though to some extent touched by the new humanism, belong fundamentally to the medieval tradition. The direct influence of the Italian Renaissance enters English poetry with the work of **Sir Thomas Wyatt** (1503–42). Wyatt's three satires are written in the *terza rima* metre, and are the first examples of it in English. The rhyme scheme is *aba; bcb . . . xyz; y*. This is the metre of Dante's *Divine Comedy*. As we have said, there was a tendency (during the Renaissance period) to regard this latter poem, because of the fierce denunciations it contains of papal and ecclesiastical corruption, as primarily satirical. Hence **Ariosto** (1474–1533) and others adopted the *terza rima* as a vehicle for satire. The second of Wyatt's satires is an abridged imitation of the tenth satire of the Italian poet **Luigi Alimanni** (1495–1556). The third satire is suggested by the fifth satire of Horace, while the first tells the well known fable of the town mouse and the country mouse. This also occurs in Horace, but had already been treated in English by the Scottish poet **Robert Henryson** (1430?–1506). All three satires deal with the characteristically Horatian theme of the inconveniences of town or court life contrasted with country retirement:

> I am not now in France to judge the wine;
> With savory sauce those delicates to feel;
> Nor yet in Spain, where one must him incline
> Rather than to be, outwardly to seem.
> I meddle not with wits that be so fine;
> Nor Flander's cheer lets not my sight to deem
> Of black and white, nor takes my wits away
> With beastliness; such do those beasts esteem.
> Nor I am not, where truth is given in prey
> For money, poison, and treason, at Rome
> A common practice, used night and day;
> But I am here in Kent and Christendom,
> Among the Muses, where I read and rhyme;
> Where if thou list, mine own John Poins, to come,
> Thou shalt be judge how I do spend my time.

In the first satire, the country mouse is amusingly characterized:

> My mother's maids, when they do sew and spin,
> They sing a song made of the fieldish mouse:
> That for because her livelode was but thin,
> Would needs go see her townish sister's house.
> She thought herself endured to grievous pain;
> The stormy blast her cave so sore did souse,
> That when the furrows swimmèd with the rain,
> She must lie cold and wet, in sorry plight;
> And worse than that, bare meat there did remain
> To comfort her, when she her house had dight.
> Sometime a barley corn, sometime a bean,
> For which she laboured hard both day and night
> In harvest time, while she might go and glean:
> And when her store was stroyed with the flood,
> Then wellaway! for she undone was clean:
> Then was she fain to take, instead of food,
> Sleep if she might, her hunger to beguile.
> 'My sister' quod she, hath a living good;
> And hence from me dwelleth not a mile.
> In cold and storm, she lieth warm and dry
> In bed of down; the dirt doth not defile

Her tender foot; she labours not as I.
Richly she feeds, and at the rich man's cost;
And for her meat she needs not crave nor cry:
By sea, by land, of delicates the most
Her cater seeks, and spareth for no peril:
She feedeth on boiled bacon-meat, and roast,
And hath thereof neither charge nor travail.
And, when she list, the liquor of the grape
Doth glad her heart, till that her belly swell.

The reception she receives from her sister, however, should have warned her that town life has its drawbacks:

And to the door now is she come by stealth,
And with her foot anon she scrapes full fast
The other for fear durst not well scarce appear,
Of every noise so was the wretch aghast.
At last she asked softly who was there,
And in her language as well as she could,
'Peep', quod the other, 'Sister I am here'.
'Peace', quod the town-mouse, 'why speakest thou so loud?'
And by the hand she took her fair and well.
'Welcome', quod she, 'my Sister, by the rood'.

She is in for a rude shock when the cat puts in an appearance.

The Steele Glas by the early Elizabethan poet **George Gascoigne** (1525?–77) is one of the earliest original poems written in blank verse. This metre, of Italian origin, had been first introduced by Wyatt's younger contemporary **Henry Howard, Earl of Surrey** (1517?–47) in his translation of part of the *Aeneid.* Nevertheless *The Steele Glas* belongs more to the Middle Ages than to the Renaissance. As its title suggests its aim is to hold up the mirror to the whole of the society of its time, of which it takes a pessimistic view. It owes something to the tradition of Langland's *Piers Plowman.* In the following passage the same symbolic figure is introduced:

Behold him, priests, and though he stink of sweat,
Disdain him not: for shall I tell you what?
Such climb to heaven before the shaven crowns:
But how? forsooth with true humility.
Not that they hoard their grain when it is cheap,
Nor that they kill the calf to have the milk,
Nor that they set debate between their lords,
By earing up the balks that part their bounds:

Nor for because they can both crouch and creep
(The guileful'st men that ever God yet made)
When as they mean most mischief and deceit,
Nor that they can cry out on landlords loud,
And say they rack their rents an ace too high,
When they themselves do sell their landlord's lamb
For greater price than ewe was wont be worth.
(I see you, Piers, my glass was lately scoured.)
But for they feed with fruits of their great pains
Both king and knight and priests in cloister pent:
Therefore I say that sooner some of them
Shall scale the walls which lead us up to heaven,
Than cornfed beasts, whose belly is their God,
Although they preach of more perfection.

Edmund Spenser (1552?–99) regarded Chaucer as his master. Essentially, he was of a rather different poetical temperament: the Platonic idealism of *The Faerie Queene* is far removed from the broad humane realism of Chaucer. But in *Mother Hubbard's Tale* he really does come close to Chaucer's manner. The poem is in the form of a beast fable, like Chaucer's *Nun's Priest's Tale*. The Fox and the Ape set out to seek their fortunes. First of all they take service with a farmer, the Ape as a shepherd, with the Fox as his sheepdog; they of course take the opportunity to prey on the flock. After that they meet a priest, who advises them on how to rise in the world, and they then repair to court. Later, finding the Lion asleep, they steal his skin, and the Ape usurps his royal power. Eventually their tyrannical misgovernment arouses the wrath of Jupiter, who sends Mercury to awaken the Lion. The poem is a bitter comment on the ways of the world, and especially on the intrigues of courtiers. The Fox is Lord Burleigh, and the poem is said to have earned Spenser his lasting resentment. The Ape is a double portrait – he suggests both the Duke of Alençon, the French prince who was for a time a suitor for Queen Elizabeth's hand, and his agent Simier (Latin *simia* = ape). Here is the priest's advice on how to obtain a benefice:

First, therefore, when ye have in handsome wise
Your selfe attired, as you can devise,
Then to some Noble man your selfe applye,
Or other great one in the worldēs eye,
That hath a zealous disposition
To God, and so to his religion.
There must thou fashion eke a godly zeale,
Such as no carpers may contrayre reveale;

For each thing fained, ought more warie bee.
There thou must walke in sober gravitee,
And seeme as Saintlike as Saint *Radegund*:
Fast much, pray oft, looke lowly on the ground,
And unto everie one doo curtesie meeke:
These lookes (nought saying) doo a benefice seeke,
And be thou sure one not to lacke ere long.
But if thee list unto the Court to throng,
And there to hunt after the hopēd prey,
Then must thou thee dispose another way:
For there thou needs must learne to laugh, to lie,
To face, to forge, to scoffe, to companie,
To crouche, to please, to be a beetle stock
Of thy great Masters will, to scorne, or mock:
So maist thou chaunce mock out a Benefice,
Unlesse thou canst one conjure by device,
Or cast a figure for a Bishoprick:
And if one could, it were but a schoole-trick.

Arrived at court the Fox and the Ape soon learn to adapt their behaviour to the tone of the place:

So well they shifted, that the Ape anon
Himselfe had cloathed like a Gentleman,
And the slie Foxe, as like to be his groome,
That to the Court in seemly sort they come;
Where the fond Ape himselfe uprearing hy
Upon his tiptoes, stalketh stately by,
As if he were some great *Magnifico*,
And boldlie doth amongst the boldest go.
And his man Reynold with fine counterfesaunce
Supports his credite and his countenaunce.

The ten-syllable couplet, of course, derives from Chaucer. But Spenser here uses it for the first time as a vehicle for formal satire, for which, in the seventeenth and eighteenth centuries, it was to become the most usual metre. Spenser's handling of it to some extent prefigures the concision and point of Dryden.

3

The Jacobeans

During the later years of Queen Elizabeth's reign and that of James I a marked change came over the tone of English society and English literature. Elizabethan society had been predominantly optimistic and extrovert. The Jacobean colour is darker, and the mood more inward looking. A note of disillusion, cynicism, and melancholy is dominant. The period opens with some of Shakespeare's darker plays, such as *Hamlet*, *Measure for Measure* and *Troilus and Cressida*. The last of these, together with *Timon of Athens*, is largely satirical in tone; and satire, as a distinct *genre*, now underwent a definite vogue, which reflected the changed outlook of the age. The sources of this change are doubtless complex, and difficult to define. They must be sought in the altering social and economic circumstances of the time. The rather uninspiring personality of James I, and the altered tone which it gave to the court, probably also played a part. But the tendency of the Whig historians of the nineteenth century to make the character of the monarch the sole cause is an over-simplification. The change seems to have begun some years before the queen's death, and so also did the fashion for satire.[1] By 1599 it had become so strong that the Archbishop of Canterbury and the Bishop of London ordered a number of works to be publicly burned. These included the epigrams of **Sir John Davies** (1565?–1618), as well as Donne's and Hall's satires (though the latter were reprieved).

Thomas Lodge (1558?–1625) published his *A Fig for Momus* in 1595. This is a collection of satires in the Horatian manner. But the new satirists of the Jacobean period such as Donne, Marston and Hall took Juvenal and Persius, rather than Horace, as their models.[2] These Latin authors, as we have seen, do not employ the urbane conversational manner of Horace, but are frequently violent, harsh and obscure. The English satirists of the seventeenth century, before the time of Dryden, therefore thought it proper to exhibit a deliberate roughness in versification and obscurity of expression.

[1]In the earlier Elizabethan period **Thomas Nash** (1567–1601) exhibited considerable satirical power. But it is to be seen in his prose pamphlets rather than his verse.

[2]The influence of the satirical epigrams of **Martial** (40 B.C.–A.D. 104) is also important at this time.

This is very noticeably the case with the satires of **John Donne** (1572–1631), which belong to the earliest part of his poetical career. Though they are written in the couplet, it is treated with the utmost freedom, both in the matter of run-on lines and of stress. This later prompted Pope to 'versify' some of Donne's satires, i.e. to rewrite them in regular heroic couplets. It was largely the satires which gained for Donne's poetry in general a reputation for roughness and obscurity which led to its being almost universally under-valued and neglected for nearly three centuries after his death. To the modern ear, used to more freely stressed rhythms, Donne's satires often seem very effective. They are packed with thought, but also vivid and dramatic in their observation of contemporary life. In the first satire we find Donne encountering a tiresome foppish acquaintance in the street:

> Now leaps he upright, joggs me, and cries, 'Do you see
> Yonder well-favoured youth?' 'Which?' 'O, 'tis he
> That dances so divinely'. 'O', said I,
> 'Stand still, must you dance here for company?'
> He droop'd, we went, till one – which did excel
> Th' Indians in drinking his tobacco well –
> Met us; they talk'd; I whisper'd, 'Let us go,
> 'T may be you smell him not; truly I do'.
> He hears not me, but on the other side
> A many-coloured peacock having spied,
> Leaves him and me; I for my lost sheep stay;
> He follows, overtakes, goes on the way,
> Saying, 'Him whom I last left, all repute
> For his device in handsoming a suit,
> To judge of lace, pink, panes, print, cut, and pleat,
> Of all the court to have the best conceit.'

In the fourth satire we find a rather similar scene, rendered in an equally lifelike manner:

> Toughly and stubbornly I bear this cross; but th' hour
> Of mercy now was come; he tries to bring
> Me to pay a fine to 'scape his torturing,
> And says, 'Sir, can you spare me?' – I said, 'Willingly';
> 'Nay, sir, can you spare me a crown?' Thankfully I
> Gave it, as ransom; but as fiddlers, still,
> Though they be paid to be gone, yet needs will
> Thrust one more jig upon you; so did he
> With his long complimental thanks vex me.
> But he is gone, thanks to his needy want,

And the prerogative of my crown; scant
His thanks were ended, when I – which did see
All the court fill'd with more strange things than he –
Ran from thence with such, or more haste than one
Who fears more actions doth make from prison.

Two of Donne's satires are more philosophical in character, dealing with the subjects which were the main preoccupations of his other poetry, love and religion. The tone of the sixth satire is not unlike that of some of Donne's love poems:

Men write that love and reason disagree,
But I ne'er saw't express'd as 'tis in thee.
Well, I may lead thee, God must make thee see,
But, thine eyes blind too, there's no hope for thee.
Thou say'st she's wise and witty, fair and free;
All these are reasons why she should scorn thee.
Thou dost protest thy love, and wouldst it show
By matching her as she would match her foe;
And wouldst persuade her to a worse offence,
Than that whereof thou didst accuse her wench.
Reason there's none for thee, but thou mayst vex
Her with example. Say, for fear her sex
Shun her, she needs must change; I do not see
How reason e'er can bring that 'must' to thee.

The third satire which discusses the subject of religion has considerable subtlety of thought as well as personal feeling. It expresses the scepticism and doubts about the conflicting claims of different forms of Christianity which beset Donne's mind in the period between his abandonment of the Roman Catholic allegiance of his family and his taking Anglican orders:

Seek true religion, O where? Mirreus,
Thinking her unhoused here and fled from us,
Seeks her at Rome, there, because he doth know
That she was there a thousand years ago;
He loves her rags so, as we here obey
The state-cloth where the prince sate yesterday.
Crants to such brave loves will not be enthrall'd,
But loves her only who at Geneva's called
Religion, plain, simple, sullen, young,
Contemptuous yet unhandsome; as among
Lecherous humours, there is one that judges
No wenches wholesome, but coarse country drudges.

Graius stays still at home here, and because
Some preachers, vile ambitious bawds, and laws
Still new like fashions, bid him think that she
Which dwells with us, is only perfect, he
Embraceth her, whom his godfathers will
Tender to him, being tender; as wards still
Take such wives as their guardians offer, or
Pay values. Careless Phrygius doth abhor
All, because all cannot be good; as one,
Knowing some women whores, dares marry none.
Gracchus loves all as one, and thinks that so
As women do in divers countries go
In divers habits, yet are still one kind,
So doth, so is religion; and this blind-
Ness too much light breeds. But unmoved thou
Of force must one, and forced but one allow;
And the right.

Donne's answer, at least for the time being, would appear to be given in the following passage:

Though Truth and Falsehood be
Near twins, yet Truth a little elder is.
Be busy to seek her; believe me this,
He's not of none, nor worst, that seeks the best.
To adore, or scorn an image, or protest,
May all be bad. Doubt wisely; in strange way,
To stand inquiring right, is not to stray;
To sleep, or run wrong, is. On a huge hill,
Cragged and steep, Truth stands, and he that will
Reach her, about must and about must go,
And what th' hill's suddenness resists, win so.
Yet strive so, that before age, death's twilight,
Thy soul rest, for none can work in that night.

Besides these seven formal satires Donne wrote, but did not complete, a long satirical narrative, in Spenserian stanzas, *The Progress Of The Soul.* This makes use of the idea of transmigration. It presumably belongs to the period when Donne was still a Roman Catholic. It tells the story of the soul of Eve's apple, which was to pass through the bodies of various heretics, and end in that of Queen Elizabeth.

John Marston (1575?–1634) made the cynical and satirical stance his dominant poetic *persona*. His attitude is fundamentally a moral one, and like Donne he also eventually took holy orders. As a dramatist he established, in his play *The Malcontent*, a theatrical type which became typical of much early seventeenth-century drama and was widely imitated. The Malcontent (who in Marston's play is, like Hamlet, a prince wrongfully deprived of his inheritance, who eventually avenges himself) pinpoints the social malaise of his time. He assumes the mask of the cynic philosopher as the Renaissance understood it, and comments with bitter sarcasm on the corruption he sees around him. This is also the approach of Marston in his non-dramatic satires. The model is evidently Juvenal, and the tone is deliberately harsh and often rather unpleasant. He uses the couplet with less freedom than Donne, and the obscurity arises not so much from density of thought as from the nature of the language. Marston is one of those who affected new and often bizarre words, coined from the Latin – 'inkhornisms', as they were called. For this he was castigated by Ben Jonson in his satirical comedy *The Poetaster.*

In the *Proemium* to the first book of *The Scourge of Villainie* Marston states as it were his programme:

> I beare the scourge of iust *Rhamnusia*,
> Lashing the lewdness of *Britania*.
> Let others sing as their good *Genius* moves,
> Of deepe desines, or else of clipping loves.
> Faire fall them all, that with wits industry,
> Doe cloath good subiects in true poesie.
> But as for me, my vexed thoughtfull soule,
> Takes pleasure, in displeasing sharp controule.
> *Thou nursing Mother of faire wisedoms lore,*
> *Ingenuous Melancholy*, I implore
> Thy grave assistance, take thy gloomie seate,
> Inthrone thee in my blood; Let me intreate
> Stay his quick iocond skips, and force him runne
> A sadde pac'd course, untill my whips be done.
> *Daphne*, unclip thine armes from my sad brow,
> Blacke Cypresse crowne me whilst I up do plow
> The hidden entrailes of ranke villainie.
> Tearing the vaile from damn'd Impietie.
> Quake guzzell dogs, that live on putred slime,
> Skud from the lashes of my yerking rime.

Marston has a thoroughly pessimistic view of human nature, and imputes to the society of his time the most horrid vices. Sometimes one wonders whether this is not more literary than authentic, the vices being rather those of Juvenal's Rome than of Jacobean London. In relation to the religious controversies of the age, Marston is bitterly scornful of Puritans and Roman Catholics alike. The seventh satire of *The Scourge of Villainie* is entitled 'A Cynicke Satire' and opens with a general denunciation of humanity:

> *A man, a man, a kingdome for a man.*
> Why how now currish mad *Athenian*?
> Thou Cynick dogge, see'st not streets do swarme
> With troupes of men? No, no, for *Circes* charme
> Hath turn'd them all to swine: I never shall
> Thinke those same *Samian* sawes aunthenticall,
> But rather I dare sweare, the soules of swine
> Doe live in men, for that same radiant shine,
> That lustre wherewith natures *Nature* decked
> Our intellectuall part, that glosse is soyled
> With stayning spots of vile impietie,
> And muddy durt of sensualitie,
> These are no men, but *Apparitions,*
> *Ignes fatui, Glowormes, Fictions,*
> *Meteors, Ratts of Nilus, Fantasies,*
> *Colosses, Pictures, Shades, Resemblances.*

Immediately after this passage comes a description of a foppish gallant of the time. It will be noted, however, that although Marston was a man of the theatre, he scarcely possesses Donne's power of bringing the characters of his satires to life:

> Seest thou yon gallant in the sumptuous clothes,
> How brisk, how spruce, how gorgiously he showes,
> Note his French-herring bones, but note no more,
> Unlesse thou spy his fayre appendant whore
> That lackyes him. Marke nothing but his clothes,
> His new stampt complement, his Cannon oathes.
> Marke those, for naught but such lewd viciousnes
> Ere graced him, save Sodom beastlines.
> Is this a *Man*? Nay, an incarnate devill,
> That struts in vice, and glorieth in evill.
> *A man, a man*: peace Cynick, yon is one,
> A compleat soule, of all perfection.
> What? mean'st thou him that walks al open brested?
> Drawne through the eare with Ribands, plumy crested?
> He that doth snort in fat-fed luxury,
> And gapes for some grinding Monopoly?
> He that in effeminate invention,

In beastly source of all pollution,
In ryot, lust, and fleshly seeming sweetnes,
Sleepes sound secure, under the shade of greatnes?
Mean'st thou that sencelesse, sensuall Epicure?
That sinck of filth, that guzzell most impure?
What he? *Linceus* on my word thus presume,
He's nought but clothes, & senting sweet perfume.

Marston's scorn sometimes expresses itself in imagery of a disgusting nature, though its power cannot be denied:

O stay, thou impious slave,
Teare not the lead from off thy Fathers grave,
To stop base brokage, sell not thy fathers sheete,
His leaden sheete, that strangers eyes may greete
Both putrefaction of thy greedie Sire,
And thy abhorred viperous desire.
But wilt thou needes shall thy Dads lackie brat
Weare thy Sires halfe-rot finger in his hat?

A loathing of sex is also a prominent feature; in the following passage Marston ridicules the conventional love poetry of the time. The opening echoes Catullus' famous lines on the death of Lesbia's sparrow, and Ovid on Corinna's parrot:

Curio, aye me! thy mistres Monkey's dead,
Alas, alas, her pleasures buried.
Goe womans slave, performe his exequies,
Condole his death in mournfull Elegies.
Tut, rather Peans sing, *Hermaphrodite*,
For that sad death gives life to thy delight.
Sweet fac'd *Corinna*, daine the riband tie
Of thy Cork-shooe, or els thy slave will die:
Some puling Sonnet toles his passing bell,
Some sighing Elegie must ring his knell,
Unlesse bright sunshine of thy grace revive
His wambling stomack, certes he will dive
Into the whirle-poole of devouring death,
And to some Mermaid sacrifice his breath.
Then oh, *oh then*, to thy eternal shame,
And to the honour of sweet *Curios* name,
This Epitaph upon the Marble stone,
Must fayre be grav'd of that true loving one;

Heere lyeth hee, hee lyeth heere,
  that bounced, and pitty cryed,
The doore not op'd, fell sicke alas,
  alas fell sicke, and dyed.

Joseph Hall (1574–1656), who became Bishop of Exeter and subsequently of Norwich, was a literary rival of Marston, who glances at him in some of his satires. Hall was ambitious to be accounted the 'second English satirist'. He probably considered the first to be Spenser, in *Mother Hubbard's Tale*, since he pays tribute to the poet of *The Faerie Queene*, and his own diction and versification exhibit Spenserian influence. He also refers to Chaucer, and in one passage to 'angry Skelton's breathless rhymes'. His satires are divided into 'toothless' satires and 'biting' satires. The toothless satires are probably intended to be Horatian. They are lighter in tone and deal mostly with general topics. The biting satires are harsher and sometimes deliberately obscure. They also aim at personalities, though these are not given their true names. Among the more interesting of the toothless satires are those in which Hall discusses contemporary literary fashions. The following passage gives his opinion of the stage tragedies of the time:

One higher pitch'd doth set his soaring thought
On crowned kings, that Fortune hath low brought:
Or some upreared, high-aspiring swaine,
As it might be the Turkish Tamberlaine:
Then weeneth he his base drink-drowned spright,
Rapt to the threefold loft of heaven's height,
When he conceives upon his faigned stage
The stalking steps of his great personage,
Graced with huff-cap terms and thundring threats,
That his poor hearers' hair quite upright sets.

. . . .

The dead-struck audience, 'midst the silent rout,
Comes leaping in a self-misformed lout,
And laughs, and grins, and frames his mimic face,
And justles straight into the prince's place;
Then doth the theatre echo all aloud,
With gladsome noise of that applauding crowd.

. . . .

Meanwhile our poets in high parliament
Sit watching every word and gesturement,
Like curious censors of some doughty gear,
Whispering their verdict in their fellow's ear.

Woe to the word whose margent in their scrole
Is noted with a black condemning coal!

The eighth satire of the first book of the Toothless Satires attacks the poetry of the Roman Catholic poet and martyr Robert Southwell.

Hence, ye profane! mell not with holy things
That Sion's Muse from Palestina brings.
Parnassus is transform'd to Sion Hill,
And Jury-palms her steep ascents done fill.
Now good St. Peter weeps pure Helicon,
And both the Maries make a music moan:
Yea, and the prophet of the heav'nly lyre,
Great Solomon, sings in the English Quire;
And is become a new-found sonnetist,
Singing his love, the Holy Spouse of Christ:
Like as she were some light-skirts of the rest,
In mightiest inkhornisms he can thither wrest.
Ye Sion Muses shall by my dear will,
For this your zeal and far-admired skill,
Be straight transported from Jerusalem,
Unto the holy house of Bethlehem.

Other objects of Hall's satire include astrologers, lawyers and place-seeking churchmen. The brief sixth satire of the second book sketches the fate of the clergyman who takes a post as domestic chaplain and private tutor:

A gentle squire would gladly entertaine
Into his house some trencher-chaplaine;
Some willing man that might instruct his sons,
And that would stand to good conditions.
First that he lie upon the truckle-bed,
Whiles his young maister lieth o'er his head.
Second, that he do, on no default,
Ever presume to sit above the salt.
Third, that he never change his trencher twise.
Fourth, that he use all common courtesies;
Sit bare at meals, and one halfe rise and wait.
Last, that he never his young maister beat,
But he must aske his mother to define,
How manie jerkes she would his breech should line.
All these observ'd, he could contented bee,
To give five markes and winter liverie.

The Biting Satires contain some vivid and amusing character sketches, such as that of Virginius, the confirmed bachelor who falls in love too late:

> Virginius vow'd to keep his maiden-head,
> And eats chast lettice, and drinks poppy-seed,
> And smells on camphire fasting; and, that done,
> Long hath he liv'd, chaste as a vailed nunne;
> Free as a new-absolved damosell,
> That Frere Cornelius shrived in his cell:
> Till, now he wax'd a toothlesse bachelor,
> He thaws like Chaucer's frosty Janivere;
> And sets a month's mind upon smiling May,
> And dyes his beard that did his age bewray;
> Biting on annys-seede and rose-marine,
> Which might the fume of his rot lungs refine:
> Now he in Charon's barge a bride doth seeke,
> The maidens mocke, and call him withered leeke,
> That with a green tayle hath a hoary head;
> And now he would, and now he cannot wed.

This passage refers to Chaucer's *Merchant's Tale* of January and May. Lolio, the miser, pinches himself in order that his son may be educated as a gentleman at the Inns of Court. Hall foresees what, in a few generations, will be the result of this:

> Now I fore-see in many ages past,
> When Lolio's caytive name is quite defa'st,
> Thine heir, thine heir's heir, and his heir again
> From out the loins of careful Lolian,
> Shall climb up to the chancell pewes on high,
> And rule and raigne in their rich tenancy;
> When perch'd aloft to perfect their estate,
> They rack their rents unto a treble rate;
> And hedge in all the neighbour common lands,
> And clodge their slavish tenants with commands;
> Whiles they, poor souls, with feeling sigh complaine,
> And wish old Lolio were alive againe,
> And praise his gentle soule and wish it well,
> And of his friendly facts full often tell.
> His father dead! tush, no it was not he,
> He finds records of his great pedigree;
> And tells how first his famous ancestor
> Did come in long since with the Conqueror.
> Nor hath some bribed herald first assign'd

His quartered arms and crest of gentle kind;
The Scottish Barnacle, if I might choose,
That, of a worme, doth waxe a winged goose.
Nathlesse some hungry squire, for hope of good,
Matches the churl's sonne into gentle blood;
Whose sonne more justly of his gentry boasts,
Than who were borne at two pide-painted posts,
And had some traunting merchant to his syre,
That traffick'd both by water and by fyre.

Hall in fact shows considerable insight into the society of his time, discussing the evils of usury, of war and enclosures, as well as the rise of new social classes. In the following passage he treats of another very characteristic feature of the age – the desire for travel, and the excitement of the discoveries in the New World:

The brain-sick youth, that feeds his tickled ear
With sweet-sauced lies of some false traveller,
Which hath the Spanish Decades read awhile,
Or whet-stone leasings of old Maundeville;
Now with discourses breaks his mid-night sleepe,
Of his adventures through the Indian deepe,
Of all their massy heapes of golden mine,
Or of the antique toombs of Palestine;
Or of Damascus' magick wall of glasse,
Of Solomon his sweating piles of brasse,
Of the bird Ruc that bears an elephant,
Of mermaids that the southerne seas do haunt,
Of headless men, of savage cannibals,
The fashions of their lives and governals:
What monstrous cities there erected be,
Cayro, or the city of the Trinity.
Now are they dung-hill cocks, that have not seene
The bordering Alpes, or else the neighbour Rhene:
And now he plies the newes-full grashopper,
Of voyages and ventures to enquire.
His land mortgag'd, he sea-beat in the way,
Wishes for home a thousand sithes a day.

It will be noticed that in Hall the couplet is already beginning to be used in the closed, antithetical manner which was later to be perfected by Dryden and Pope.

As a kind of epilogue to this chapter we may quote three of the sonnets of **John Milton** (1608–74) in which the tone is really satirical. In using the sonnet for this purpose, Milton had Italian precedents. The language here approaches the roughness and colloquial character which had come to be associated with satire. It may be thought that the intended lightness of tone of the first two of these was not really Milton's forte, and that it assorts ill with the grave formality of the syntax. But the poems are not without interest. The first of these, directed against those who complained at the learned title of Milton's divorce pamphlet *Tetrachordon*, is remarkable for the ingenuity of its rhyming:

> A Book was writ of late call'd *Tetrachordon*;
> And wov'n close, both matter, form and stile;
> The Subject new: it walk'd the Town a while,
> Numbring good intellects; now seldom por'd on.
> Cries the stall-reader, bless us! what a word on
> A title page is this! and some in file
> Stand spelling fals, while one might walk to Mile-
> End Green. Why is it harder Sirs then Gordon,
> Colkitto, or Macdonnel, or Galasp?
> Those rugged names to our like mouths grow sleek
> That would have made *Quintilian* stare and gasp.
> Thy age, like ours, O soul of Sir *John Cheek*,
> Hated not Learning wors then Toad or Asp;
> When thou taught'st *Cambridge*, and King *Edward* Greek.

The next sonnet was also prompted by the adverse reception of one of Milton's pamphlets advocating reform:

> I did but prompt the age to quit their cloggs
> By the known rules of antient libertie,
> When strait a barbarous noise environs me
> Of Owles and Cuckoes, Asses, Apes and Doggs.
> As when those Hinds that were transform'd to Froggs
> Raild at *Latona's* twin-born progenie
> Which after held the Sun and Moon in fee.
> But this is got by casting Pearl to Hoggs;
> That bawle for freedom in their senseless mood,
> And still revolt when truth would set them free.
> Licence they mean when they cry libertie;
> For who loves that, must first be wise and good;
> But from that mark how far they roave we see
> For all this wast of wealth, and loss of blood.

Latona was the mother of Apollo and Diana. Some peasants who mocked at her, in her wanderings on earth pursued by Juno's jealous anger, were turned into frogs.

The sonnet *On the new forcers of Conscience under the Long Parliament* has a more public reference:

Because you have thrown off your Prelate Lord,
 And with stiff Vowes renounc'd his Liturgie
 To seise the widdow'd whore Pluralitie
 From them whose sin ye envi'd, not abhor'd,
Dare ye for this adjure the Civill Sword
 To force our Consciences that Christ set free,
 And ride us with a classic Hierarchy
 Taught ye by meer *A.S.* and *Rotherford?*
Men whose Life, Learning, Faith and pure intent
 Would have been held in high esteem with *Paul*
 Must now be nam'd and printed Hereticks
By shallow *Edwards* and Scotch what d'ye call:
 But we do hope to find out all your tricks,
 Your plots and packings wors then those of *Trent*,
  That so the Parliament
May with their wholsom and preventive Shears
Clip your Phylacteries, though bauk your Ears,
  And succour our just Fears
When they shall read this clearly in your charge
New Presbyter is but *Old Priest* writ Large.

Metrically this poem is a regular sonnet on the Italian model, but with two codas added.

4

The Restoration

We have now reached what may be considered as the classical age of English satire, which extends from Dryden's time to the end of the eighteenth century. Dryden was to create what was virtually a new type of satire, urbane and ironic in tone, instead of relying on violence of language and coarseness of abuse. At the same time he abandoned that metrical roughness which his Jacobean predecessors had considered appropriate to this kind of poetry, and developed the balanced, epigrammatic and antithetical heroic couplet which was to be the characteristic verse form of the Augustan age. Although we associate the heroic couplet, in this form, largely with satire, it should be noted that it is so called because it was considered to be the English equivalent of the Latin hexameter (originally of Greek origin) as the standard metre for heroic (i.e. epic) poetry. But the hexameter had also been the metre employed by the Latin satirists.

We have already seen a certain tendency in the earlier seventeenth century towards using the couplet as a closed, self-contained unit, avoiding *enjambement*, and towards antithesis and balance within the line itself. This development is generally associated with the names of **Sir John Denham** (1615–69) and **Edmund Waller** (1606–87). They are comparatively minor poets, and in the field of satire contributed little; but in the age which followed their deaths they were commonly reckoned as the first 'reformers of our numbers'. Pope was only repeating a commonplace of his period when he characterized Dryden's line as one in which 'Denham's strength and Waller's sweetness join'. Before considering Dryden's achievement, however, it will be necessary to examine the work of two satirists who continued the earlier tradition of metaphysical verse into the Restoration period. These are Marvell and Butler. They however, resemble Dryden, and differ from the Jacobean satirists, in that their work deals less with moral and social generalities than with the party political and religious animosities of their time.

Andrew Marvell (1621–78) turned from lyrical and pastoral poetry to satire during the Restoration period, though his *Character of Holland* belongs earlier. Marvell had held aloof during the Civil War, but under

Charles II, as Member of Parliament for Hull, he was deeply involved in opposition to the policies of the King.

The *Character of Holland* was written under the Commonwealth, in the context of Oliver Cromwell's successful naval wars against the Dutch. It is a light-hearted and extravagantly witty view of the Dutch people and of their country:

> *Holland*, that scarce deserves the name of *Land*,
> As but th' Off-scouring of the *Brittish Sand*;
> And so much Earth as was contributed
> By *English Pilots* when they heav'd the Lead;
> Or what by th'Oceans slow alluvion fell,
> Of shipwrackt Cockle and the Muscle-shell;
> This indigested vomit of the Sea
> Fell to the *Dutch* by just Propriety.
> Glad then, as Miners that have found the Oar,
> They with mad labour fish'd the *Land* to *Shoar*;
> And div'd as desperately for each piece
> Of Earth, as if't had been of *Ambergreece*;
> Collecting anxiously small Loads of Clay,
> Less than what building Swallows bear away;
> Or then those Pills which sordid Beetles roul,
> Transfusing into them their Dunghil Soul.
> How did they rivet, with Gigantick Piles,
> Thorough the Center their new-catched Miles;
> And to the stake a strugling Country bound,
> Where barking Waves still bait the forced Ground;
> Building their *watry Babel* far more high
> To reach the *Sea*, then those to scale the *Sky*.

Marvell's satires written in the reign of Charles II, on the other hand, are informed by a savage indignation. *The Last Instructions to a Painter* follows a procedure which had been originated by Waller, and had been used by Denham. The poet imagines that he is addressing a painter who is to depict the age in its true colours. In *The Last Instructions to a Painter* the moral corruption of society is typified, among others, by the King's mistress, the notorious Lady Castlemaine:

> Paint *Castlemaine* in Colours that will hold,
> Her, not her Picture, for she now grows old.
> She through her Lacquies Drawers as he ran,
> Discern'd Love's Cause, and a new Flame began.
> Her wonted joys thenceforth and *Court* she shuns,

And still within her mind the Footman runs:
His brazen Calves, his brawny Thighs, (the Face
She slights) his Feet shapt for a smoother race.
Poring within her Glass she re-adjusts
Her looks, and oft-try'd Beauty now distrusts:
Fears lest he scorn a Woman once assay'd,
And now first, wisht she e're had been a Maid.
Great Love, how dost thou triumph, and how reign,
That to a Groom couldst humble her disdain!
Stript to her Skin, see how she stooping stands,
Nor scorns to rub him down with those fair Hands;
And washing (lest the scent her Crime disclose)
His sweaty Hooves, tickles him 'twixt the Toes.
But envious Fame, too soon, begun to note
More gold in's Fob, more Lace upon his Coat
And he, unwary, and of Tongue too fleet,
No longer could conceal his Fortune sweet.
Justly the Rogue was whipt in Porter's Den:
And *Jermyn* straight has leave to come agen.
Ah *Painter*, now could *Alexander* live,
And this *Campaspe* thee *Apelles* give!

From this, Marvell leads on to political corruption, and especially the shameful neglect of the Navy, so that a Dutch fleet could sail with impunity up the Medway:

Ruyter the while, that had our Ocean curb'd,
Sail'd now among our Rivers undisturb'd:
Survey'd their Crystal Streams, and Banks so green,
And Beauties e're this never naked seen.
Through the vain sedge the bashful *Nymphs* he ey'd;
Bosomes, and all which from themselves they hide.
The Sun much brighter, and the Skies more clear,
He finds the Air, and all things, sweeter here.
The sudden change, and such a tempting sight,
Swells his old Veins with fresh Blood, fresh Delight.
Like am'rous Victors he begins to shave,
And his new Face looks in the *English* Wave.
His sporting Navy all about him swim,
And witness their complaisence in their trim.
Their streaming Silks play through the weather fair,
And with inveigling Colours Court the Air.
While the red Flags breath on their Top-masts high
Terrour and War, but want an Enemy.

The tone of this latter passage is partly playful, and suggestive of the mock heroic style. But some of Marvell's later satires are much more bitter. In *Britannia and Rawleigh* he despairs of Charles II's ever being willing to govern constitutionally, and indeed of the whole house of Stuart. The standpoint is now openly republican. The poem is in the form of a dialogue between Britannia and the great Elizabethan, who had come to be thought of as a hero of English liberty, and whom the first of the Stuarts had imprisoned and executed. In the following passage Britannia is made to denounce Charles II for making his country subservient to France, and for the scandals of his private life. The administration of the 'Cabal' is also attacked, and the Duke of York for his Roman Catholic allegiance and alleged Irish sympathies. 'The French Dame' is an allegorical figure representing France itself:

> But his fair soul, transform'd by that French Dame,
> Had lost all sense of Honour, Justice, fame;
> Like a Tame spinster in's seraglio sits,
> Besieg'd by's whores, Buffoones, and Bastard Chitts;
> Luld in security, rouling in lust,
> Resigns his Crown to Angell Carwells trust.
> Her Creature Osborn the Revenue steals;
> False Finch, Knave Anglesey misguide the seals;
> Mack James the Irish Pagod does Adore,
> His French and Teagues comand on sea and shoar.
> The scotch scabbado of one Court, two Isles,
> Fiend Lauderdale, with ordure all defiles.
> Thus the state's night-Mard by this Hellish rout
> And none are left these furyes to cast out.
> Oh Vindex, come, and purge the Poyson'd state;
> Descend, descend, ere the Cures desperate.

Samuel Butler (1612–80) is chiefly remembered as the author of one poem, *Hudibras*. Appearing soon after the Restoration its bitter satire on the Puritans gained it immediate and lasting popularity. It still recommends itself by the intellectual virtuosity of its wit, and its learning, which exhibit its descent from the metaphysical tradition, and especially from the earlier satires of **John Cleveland** (1613–58). *Hudibras* is a long burlesque narrative, written in the short or octosyllabic couplet. Butler frequently makes use of double rhymes, with deliberately grotesque effect. This device was to be much used by later writers of comic verse, such as Byron and Hood. This form of the short couplet, with burlesque rhymes, came in fact to be known as Hudibrastic verse. The plan of the poem is based on that of *Don Quixote*, though its tone is quite different. Hudibras and Ralpho ride out as knight-errant and squire to engage in a series of combats against the representatives of those popular amusements so much disliked by the Puritans, such as bear-baiting and fiddling. They also engage in long and learned theological disputes. Hudibras himself represents the Presbyterians. His grotesque appearance and character are given a lengthy description, of which the following is a part:

> For his *Religion*, it was fit
> To match his Learning and his Wit:
> 'Twas *Presbyterian* true blew,
> For he was of that stubborn Crew
> Of Errant Saints, whom all men grant
> To be the true Church *Militant*:
> Such as do build their Faith upon
> The holy Text of *Pike* and *Gun*;
> Decide all Controversies by
> Infallible *Artillery*;
> And prove their Doctrine Orthodox
> By Apostolick *Blows* and *Knocks*;
> Call Fire and Sword and Desolation,
> A *godly-thorough Reformation*,
> Which alwayes must be carry'd on,
> And still be doing, never done:
> As if Religion were intended
> For nothing else but to be mended.

Ralpho, on the other hand represents the Independents (Congregationalists). The early Independents differed more sharply from the Presbyterians than is sometimes realized. This is well brought out by Butler. Whereas Hudibras relies on his immense scholastic learning, Ralpho's interests are more esoteric, and include such subjects as alchemy and astrology, while his main appeal is to the Inner Light:

> 'Tis a *dark-Lantorn* of the Spirit,
> Which none see by but those that bear it:
> A Light that falls down from on high,
> For Spiritual Trades to cozen by:
> An *Ignis Fatuus*, that bewitches,
> And leads men into Pools and Ditches,
> To make them *dip* themseves, and sound
> For Christendom in dirty Pond;
> To dive like Wild-fowl for Salvation,

And fish to catch Regeneration.
This Light inspires, and plays upon
The nose of Saint, like Bag-pipe-drone,
And speaks through hollow empty soul,
As through a Trunk, or whisp'ring hole,
Such language as no mortal ear
But spiritual Eve-droppers can hear.

Of Butler's shorter poems one of the most interesting is *The Elephant in the Moon*. This is a satire on the members of the Royal Society which had been founded for the study of nature by the experimental methods of the new science. Its members meet to observe the moon through a great telescope. The first to look is able to give a remarkable account of the moon's inhabitants:

Quoth he, The old inhabitants o' th' Moon,
Who, when the Sun shines hottest about noon,
Are wont to live in cellars underground
Of eight miles deep, and more than eighty round,
In which at once they use to fortify
Against the sun-beams and the enemy,
Are counted borough-towns and cities there,
Because th' inhabitants are civiler
Than those rude country peasants, that are found
Like mountaineers, to live on th' upper ground,
Named Privolvans, with whom the others are
Perpetually in state of open war.
And now both armies, mortally enrag'd,
Are in a fierce and bloody fight engaged,
And many fall on both sides kill'd and slain,
As by the telescope 'tis clear and plain.
Look in it quickly then, that every one
May see his share before the battle's done.'

But a subsequent observer makes an even more startling discovery:

(And thus began) A stranger sight appears
Than ever yet was seen in all the Spheres,
A greater wonder, more unparalleled
Than ever mortal Tube, or Eye beheld;
A mighty Elephant from one of those
Two fighting armies is at length broke loose,
And with the desp'rate horror of the fight
Appears amaz'd, and in a dreadful fright;

Look quickly, lest the only sight of us
Should cause the startled creature to imboss.'

To the consternation of the learned philosophers, the elephant is eventually discovered to be a mouse which has crept into the telescope, while the Privolvans and the Subvolvans are a swarm of gnats and flies.

John Dryden (1631–1700) is one of the very great writers of English verse satire. But although it is for his satirical poems that he has been most highly praised, it should not be forgotten that he handled with distinction almost all the verse forms which were practised in his day. *Absalom and Achitophel*, the first of Dryden's satires, appeared in 1681, when he was fifty. The mastery of the heroic couplet which this poem evinces could only have been achieved after a long period of apprenticeship. In his rhymed heroic plays Dryden had learned to use the couplet for vigorous dramatic dialogue, and in *Religio Laici* as a medium for closely reasoned argument in verse. Dryden makes use of his skill in both these with great effectiveness in his satires. All three of them stem from the political crisis of the 1680s. This had been triggered off by the allegation, on the part of Titus Oates, of a supposed Popish Plot, inducing a mood of near hysteria in the Protestant masses. The Earl of Shaftesbury and his Whig associates attempted to capitalize on this by seeking to fix the succession on Charles II's illegitimate son, the Protestant Duke of Monmouth, instead of the Roman Catholic Duke of York (later James II). The sympathies of Dryden's family had been Puritan, and he had begun his poetic career with a encomiastic poem on the death of Cromwell. But at the Restoration he had accepted the royal authority as of divine right. Dryden was by temperament profoundly sceptical, and distrustful of human nature. He believed in the need for lawful authority, and suspected beyond everything the unstable passions of the mob, and the ambition of self-seeking politicians, such as he considered Shaftesbury to be. *Absalom and Achitophel* is thus written to oppose Shaftesbury's party, and to uphold the policy of the King and his Tory ministers. In form it is an epic satire. Dryden treats the story of David's rebellious son Absalom and the evil counsellor Achitophel as an analogy for the contemporary events. The poem contains echoes of Cowley's epic on King David, *The Davideis* and also of *Paradise Lost*. Achitophel is represented as a Satanic figure, and his attempt to get Absalom to break his bond of duty to his father, the Lord's Anointed, is analogous to Satan's temptation of Adam and Eve. Dryden tells the story with great narrative skill, but the most famous passages in the poem are those in which Dryden sketches the characters of the principal participants. The character, as a literary form, on the model of the Greek writer Theophrastus, was widely practised during the seventeenth century, and is here fused with the satire. Dryden's character sketches have a universality which transcends the historical particularities which gave rise to them. That of Achitophel stands for all time as the portrait of an unscrupulous power-hungry politician:

Of these the false *Achitophel* was first:
A Name to all succeeding Ages Curst.
For close Designs, and crooked Counsels fit;
Sagacious, Bold, and Turbulent of wit:
Restless, unfixt in Principles and Place;
In Pow'r unpleas'd, impatient of Disgrace.
A fiery Soul, which working out its way,
Fretted the Pigmy Body to decay:
And o'er inform'd the Tenement of Clay.
A daring Pilot in extremity;
Pleas'd with the Danger, when the Waves went high
He sought the Storms; but for a Calm unfit,
Would Steer too nigh the Sands, to boast his Wit.
Great Wits are sure to Madness near ally'd,
And thin Partitions do their Bounds divide:
Else, why should he, with Wealth and Honour blest,
Refuse his Age the needful hours of Rest?
Punish a Body which he coud not please,
Bankrupt of Life, yet Prodigal of Ease?
And all to leave, what with his Toyl he won,
To that unfeather'd, two Leg'd thing, a Son:
Got, while his Soul did hudled Notions try;
And born a shapeless Lump, like Anarchy.
In Friendship False, Implacable in Hate,
Resolv'd to Ruine or to Rule the State.

Beside this picture of Shaftesbury stands that of the Duke of Buckingham (Zimri) the dangerously unstable intellectual:

In the first Rank of these did *Zimri* stand:
A man so various, that he seem'd to be
Not one, but all Mankinds Epitome.
Stiff in Opinions, always in the wrong;
Was every thing by starts, and nothing long:
But, in the course of one revolving Moon,
Was Chymist, Fidler, States-man, and Buffoon:
Then all for Women, Painting, Rhiming, Drinking;

Besides ten thousand Freaks that dy'd in thinking.
Blest Madman, who coud every hour employ,
With something New to wish, or to enjoy!
Raling and praising were his usual Theams;
And both (to show his Judgment) in Extreams;
So over Violent, or over Civil,
That every man, with him, was God or Devil.
In squandring Wealth was his peculiar Art:
Nothing went unrewarded, but Desert.
Begger'd by Fools, whom still he found too late:
He had his Jest, and they had his Estate.
He laught himself from Court, then sought Relief
By forming Parties, but coud ne're be Chief:
For, spight of him, the weight of Business fell
On *Absalom* and wise *Achitophel*;
Thus, wicked but in will, of means bereft,
He left not Faction, but of that was left.

Dryden later wrote of this passage:

The Character of *Zimri* in my *Absalom*, is, in my Opinion, worth the whole Poem: 'Tis not bloody, but 'tis ridiculous enough. And he for whom it was intended, was too witty to resent it as an injury. If I had rail'd, I might have suffer'd for it justly: But I manag'd my own Work more happily, perhaps more dextrously. I avoided the mention of great Crimes, and apply'd my self to the representing of Blind-sides, and little extravagancies: By which, the wittier a Man is, he is generally the more obnoxious. It succeeded as I wish'd; the Jest went round, and he was laught at in his turn who began the Frolick.

In 1681 Shaftesbury was acquitted on a charge of high treason by the grand jury of the county of Middlesex. His supporters struck a medal to commemorate this. Dryden's next satire, *The Medall*, takes this as its starting point. Its object is further to discredit Shaftesbury. Unlike *Absalom and Achitophel*, *The Medall* is not narrative in form. We may consider it an example of Juvenalian satire. In *The Medall* the character of Shaftesbury is further developed. He is represented as a demagogue, flattering the people for his own ends:

He preaches to the Crowd, that Pow'r is lent,
But not convey'd to Kingly Government;
That Claimes successive bear no binding force;
That Coronation Oaths are things of course;
Maintains the Multitude can never err;
And sets the People in the Papal Chair.

The reason's obvious; *Int'rest never lyes*;
The most have still their Int'rest in their eyes;
The pow'r is always theirs, and pow'r is ever wise.
Almighty crowd, thou shorten'st all dispute;
Power is thy Essence; Wit thy Attribute!
Nor Faith nor Reason make thee at a stay,
Thou leapst o'r all Eternal truths, in thy *Pindarique* way!

The Medall also contains the most complete and positive statement of Dryden's own Tory political philosophy:

Thus Out-laws open Villany maintain:
They steal not, but in Squadrons scoure the Plain:
And, if their Pow'r the Passengers subdue;
The Most have right, the wrong is in the Few.
Such impious Axiomes foolishly they show;
For in some Soyles Republiques will not grow:
Our Temp'rate Isle will no extremes sustain,
Of pop'lar Sway, or Arbitrary Reign:
But slides between them both into the best;
Secure in freedom, in a Monarch blest.
And though the Clymate, vex't with various Winds,
Works through our yielding Bodies, on our Minds,
The wholsome Tempest purges what it breeds;
To recommend the Calmness that succeeds.

Absalom and Achitophel elicited numerous replies from poets on the Whig side. Among these was Thomas Shadwell. By an irony of fate Shadwell was to succeed Dryden as Poet Laureate when the latter, who had become a Roman Catholic, forfeited the office after the revolution of 1688. Shadwell had very little merit as a poet, though he was a competent dramatist in the tradition of Ben Jonson. In the second part of *Absalom and Achitophel*, written in collaboration with Nahum Tate, Dryden satirized Shadwell as Og. But in *Mack Flecknoe* Dryden devoted an entire satire to making his opponent look ridiculous. *Mack Flecknoe* is the first example in English of a new type of satire, the mock-heroic. This involves the application of the conventions of classical epic poetry to a trivial and ridiculous subject. *Absalom and Achitophel* is not strictly a mock-heroic poem, since in it the epic conventions are used quite seriously. There was a precedent for the mock-heroic poem in ancient poetry in *The Battle of the Frogs and Mice*. This was attributed to Homer, though it is in fact later in date than the Homeric poems. But the *genre* began to be developed in European literature during the seventeenth century. The Italian poet

Alessandro Tassoni (1565–1635) had written *La Secchia Rapita* (The Stolen Bucket). This was based on an incident in the medieval wars between Modena and Bologna, in which the Modenese carried off a bucket from a public well in Bologna. This was followed by *Le Lutrin* by the French neo-classical poet **Boileau** (1636–1711). This is a satire on the clergy, who quarrel over the possession of a lectern. In *Mack Flecknoe* Dryden represents the recently deceased poet Richard Flecknoe as appointing Shadwell his spiritual son and heir, and ruler over all the realms of Non-sense. Flecknoe had in fact been a minor poet of the metaphysical school, which was now grown thoroughly out of fashion. He was also a Roman Catholic priest, and there is therefore an added irony in associating him with 'the true blue Protestant poet' Shadwell. In this poem, Dryden created the idea of an anti-poetic realm of Dullness, with its own apostolic succession of bad poets – an idea which was to be much more fully developed by Pope in the *Dunciad*. In a passage verging on the blasphemous Dryden makes Flecknoe stand to Shadwell as John the Baptist to Christ:

> *Sh(adwell)* alone my perfect image bears,
> Mature in dullness from his tender years.
> *Sh(adwell)* alone, of all my Sons, is he
> Who stands confirm'd in full stupidity.
> The rest to some faint meaning make pretence,
> But *Sh(adwell)* never deviates into sense.
> Some Beams of Wit on other souls may fall,
> Strike through and make a lucid intervall;
> But *Sh(adwell)'s* genuine night admits no ray,
> His rising Fogs prevail upon the Day:
> Besides his goodly Fabrick fills the eye,
> And seems design'd for thoughtless Majesty:
> Thoughtless as Monarch Oakes, that shade the plain,
> And, spread in solemn state, supinely reign.
> *Heywood* and *Shirley* were but Types of thee,
> Thou last great Prophet of Tautology:
> Even I, a dunce of more renown than they,
> Was sent before but to prepare thy way:
> And coarsely clad in *Norwich* Drugget came
> To teach the Nations in thy greater name.

Dryden's views on satire are set forth in the *Discourse Concerning the Original and Progress of Satire* prefixed to a translation of Juvenal and Persius by himself and others. This lengthy essay contains perhaps the most important observations on the subject in English. It begins with some rather fulsome flattery of the Earl of Dorset, to whom the work is dedicated, and an irrelevant but interesting digression on epic poetry and the problem of 'machinery'. Dryden then goes on to give a learned, and in the main accurate, account of the origins and history of Roman satire. He proceeds to a detailed critical comparison of Persius, Horace and Juvenal. He is inclined to give the first place to the last of these, though he wins from Horace only by a short head. Juvenalian satire is considered as analogous to tragedy, since its objects are crimes and vices arising from our disordered passions; Horatian satire resembles comedy, since it deals rather with follies which are due to a defect of reason. Among his English predecessors Dryden pays tribute to the wit of Donne, though he condemns his versification, and to Butler's *Hudibras*. He takes exception, however to Butler's double rhymes, and considers the short eight-syllable couplet less convenient for satire then the ten-syllable heroic couplet.

Dryden does not give a formal definition of satire till near the end of the essay. He takes it from the German humanist critic Heinsius:

Satire is a kind of Poetry, without a Series of Action, invented for the purging of our Minds; in which Humane Vices, Ignorance, and Errors, and all things besides, which are produc'd from them, in every Man, are severely Reprehended; partly Dramatically, partly Simply, and sometimes in both kinds of speaking; but for the most part Figuratively, and Occultly; consisting in a low familiar way, chiefly in a sharp and pungent manner of Speech; but partly, also, in a Facetious and Civil way of Jesting; by which, either Hatred, or Laughter, or Indignation is mov'd.

Dryden however considers that Heinsius's words about the lowness of the style make this definition applicable only to Horatian satire. He had himself earlier in the essay more significantly said that the finest and most delicate touches of satire consist in fine raillery. He goes on to say:

How easie it is to call Rogue and Villain, and that wittily! But how hard to make a Man appear a Fool, a Blockhead, or a Knave, without using any of these opprobrious terms! To spare the grossness of the Names, and to do the thing yet more severely, is to draw a full Face, and to make the Nose and Cheeks stand out, and yet not to employ any depth of Shadowing. This is the Mystery of that Noble Trade; which yet no Master can teach to his Apprentice: He may give the Rules, but the Scholar is never the nearer in his practice. Neither is it true, that this fineness of Raillery is offensive. A witty Man is tickl'd while he is hurt in this manner; and a Fool feels it not. The occasion of an Offence may possibly be given, but he cannot take it. If it be granted that in effect this way does more Mischief; that a Man is secretly wounded, and though he be not sensible himself, yet the Malicious World will find it for him: Yet there is still a vast difference betwixt the slovenly Butchering of a Man, and the fineness of a stroak that separates the Head from the Body, and leaves it standing in its place. A man may be capable, as *Jack Ketche's* Wife said of his Servant, of a plain piece of Work, a bare Hanging; but to make a Malefactor die sweetly, was only belonging to her husband.

This is clearly Dryden's own method, and it is what differentiates his work from that of his predecessors.

Dryden also makes a distinction between satire proper and the lampoon. The lampoon, which is a personal attack on an individual, is:

a dangerous sort of Weapon, and for the most part Unlawful. We have no Moral right on the Reputation of other Men. 'Tis taking from them, what we cannot restore to them. There are only two Reasons, for which we may be permitted to write Lampoons; and I will not promise that they can always justifie us: The first is Revenge, when we have been affronted in the same Nature, or have been any ways notoriously abus'd, and can make ourselves no other Reparation. And yet we know, that, in Christian Charity, all Offences are to be forgiven; as we expect the like Pardon for those which we daily commit against Almighty God. And this Consideration has often made me tremble when I was saying our Saviour's Prayer; for the plain Condition of the forgiveness which we beg, is the pardoning of others the Offences which they have done to us: For which Reason I have many times avoided the Commission of that Fault; ev'n when I have been notoriously provok'd.

Dryden gives 'the second Reason, which may justifie a Poet, when he writes against a particular Person' as being:

when he is become a Publick Nuisance. All those, whom *Horace* in his Satires, and *Persius* and *Juvenal* have mention'd in theirs, with a Brand of infamy, are wholly such. 'Tis an Action of Virtue to make Examples of vicious Men. They may and ought to be up-braided with their Crimes and Follies: Both for their own amendment, if they are not yet incorrigible; and for the Terrour of others, to hinder them from falling into those Enormities, which they see are so severely punish'd, in the Persons of others: The first Reason was only an Excuse for Revenge: But this second is absolutely of a Poet's Office to perform: But how few Lampooners are there now living, who are capable of this Duty!

The attack on Shadwell is presumably to be justified on the first score; that on Shaftesbury and his associates on the second score.

John Oldham (1653–83) was a younger contemporary of Dryden, who commemorated his early death in some notable verses. Dryden pays tribute to the force and wit of Oldham's writing, but rightly considered his versification rough and unpolished:

O early ripe! to thy abundant Store
What could advancing Age have added more?
It might (what Nature never gives the Young)
Have taught the Numbers of thy Native Tongue.
But Satire needs not those, and Wit will shine
Through the harsh Cadence of a rugged Line.
A noble Error, and but seldom made,
When Poets are by too much force betray'd.
Thy gen'rous Fruits, though gather'd ere their prime,
Still shew'd a Quickness; and maturing Time
But mellows what we write to the dull Sweets of Rhyme.

The background of Oldham's *Satires against the Jesuits* is the Popish Plot agitation. Oldham is a violent partisan on the Whig and Protestant side, and represents the Jesuits as monsters capable of every sort of wickedness. His satires do not make very pleasant reading; they are extremely harsh and often sadistic in their imagery, but cannot be denied a certain power. The following is one of Oldham's less extreme passages:

Go, foul imposters, to some duller soil,
Some easier nation with your cheats beguile;
Where your gross common gulleries may pass,
To slur and top on bubbled consciences;
Where ignorance, and the Inquisition rules,
Where the vile herd of poor implicit fools
Are damned contentedly, where they are led
Blindfold to hell, and thank, and pay their guide!
Go, where all your black tribe before are gone,
Follow Chastel, Ravaillac, Clement down,
Your Catesby, Faux, and Garnet, thousands more,
And those who hence have lately raised the score;
Where the grand traitor now, and all the crew
Of his disciples must receive their due;
Where flames, and tortures of eternal date
Must punish you, yet ne'er can expiate:
Learn duller fiends your unknown cruelties,
Such as no wit, but yours, could e'er devise,
No guilt, but yours, deserve; make hell confess
Itself outdone, it's devils damned for less.

Rochester (1648–80) is one of the most brilliant and characteristic figures of the Restoration period. Until recently his fame as a poet was somewhat overshadowed by a reputation for indecency. This was not wholly deserved, for many of the improper poems formerly attributed to him have been shown not to be really his. He could write love lyrics which were both witty and tender. His principal satire, *A Satyr against Mankind*, though somewhat careless in versification, exhibits originality and power of thought. It opens with an attack on Reason, as the faculty supposed to differentiate mankind from the beasts:

> *Reason*, which Fifty times for one does err.
> *Reason*, an *Ignis fatuus*, in the *Mind*,
> Which leaving light of Nature, sense behind;
> Pathless and dang'rous wandring ways it takes,
> Through errors, Fenny-*Boggs*, and Thorny *Brakes*;
> Whilst the misguided follower, climbs with pain,
> *Mountains* of Whimseys, heap'd in his own *Brain*:
> Stumbling from thought to thought, falls head-long down,
> Into doubts boundless Sea, where like to drown,
> Books bear him up awhile, and makes him try,
> To swim with Bladders of *Philosophy*;
> In hopes still t'oretake the escaping light,
> The *Vapour* dances in his dazled sight,
> Till spent, it leaves him to eternal Night.
> Then Old Age, and experience, hand in hand,
> Lead him to death, and make him understand,
> After a search so painful, and so long,
> That all his Life he has been in the wrong;
> Hudled in dirt, the reas'ning Engine lyes,
> Who was so proud, so witty, and so wise.

To this speculative Reason Rochester opposes his own version of practical Reason:

> But thoughts, are giv'n for Actions government,
> Where Action ceases, thoughts impertinent:
> Our *Sphere* of Action, is lifes happiness,
> And he who thinks Beyond, thinks like an *Ass*.
> Thus, whilst 'gainst false reas'ning I inveigh,
> I own right *Reason*, which I wou'd obey:
> That *Reason* that distinguishes by sense,
> And gives us *Rules*, of good, and ill from thence:
> That bounds desires, with a reforming Will,
> To keep 'em more in vigour, not to kill.
> Your *Reason* hinders, mine helps t'enjoy,
> Renewing Appetites, yours wou'd destroy.
> My Reason is my *Friend*, yours is a *Cheat*,
> Hunger call's out, my Reason bids me eat;

Perversely yours, your Appetite does mock,
This asks for Food, that answers what's a Clock?

We perceive a lively, sceptical, and in many ways very modern intelligence at work in this poem. The intellectual background is in fact the philosophy of Thomas Hobbes.

5

The Eighteenth Century: I

Probably the greatest satirist, in any language, is **Jonathan Swift** (1667–1745). But this claim must be based primarily on his prose – such writings as *A Modest Proposal, Gulliver's Travels, A Tale of a Tub* and *The Battle of the Books*. The last of these, by the way, is to be considered as a mock-heroic poem in prose. The rules of epic poetry were held to apply, *mutatis mutandis*, to the mock-heroic. Since it was an established principle that an epic poem need not necessarily be in verse, it was quite logical of Swift to choose prose for *The Battle of the Books*.

Swift's writings in verse are extensive, but by comparison with his prose they have been neglected and sometimes underestimated. It is true that Dryden, according to Johnson, is supposed to have said: 'Cousin Swift, you will never be a poet'. If Dryden (who was a distant cousin of Swift's by marriage) really did say this, it was after reading Swift's early and not very successful attempts at the Pindaric ode. Swift's mature satirical verses have very considerable merits. These are of the same sort that we find in his prose, and present the same images – including his obsessive disgust with the physical functions of the human body. Swift almost always uses the short octosyllabic couplet, but generally without Butler's double rhymes. Nor does he follow Butler in the intellectual virtuosity of his wit. His manner, as in his prose, is lucid and without unnecessary adornment.

The literary, as well as the personal, character of Swift is, of course, controversial, and has been subject to widely differing interpretations. It may help us to understand him if we consider him as a Christian Cynic – giving to that phrase the same kind of weight as when we call Spenser a Christian Platonist, or Montaigne a Christian Sceptic. We have already seen how the Cynic *persona* played an important part in the late Renaissance, especially in satire. This tradition continued in the later seventeenth century in such figures as Alceste in Molière's *Le Misanthrope*, and Manly in Wycherley's *The Plain Dealer* which is partly based on Molière's comedy. Manly opposes a blunt masculine cynicism to the corruption and sophistication of fashionable society, but he is essentially good-hearted. Moreover he is himself also deceived. The tradition of Renaissance humanist cynicism was also continued in the *Maxims* of de la Rochefoucault to which Swift refers in the opening lines of *Verses on the Death of Dr. Swift*:

As *Rochefoucault* his Maxims drew
From Nature, I believe 'em true:
They argue no corrupted Mind
In him; the Fault is in Mankind.

This Maxim more than all the rest
Is thought too base for human Breast;
'In all distresses of our Friends
'We first consult our private Ends,
'While Nature kindly bent to ease us,
'Points out some Circumstance to please us.

We have not here sufficient space to deal with Swift's verse in detail. To represent his manner and point of view it may be enough to quote again from the *Verses on the Death of Dr. Swift*. This is one of Swift's finest poems, and may be considered as his *apologia*. It should be compared with Pope's *Epistle to Arbuthnot*. Swift imagines how his friends and his enemies alike will receive the news of his death, and then allows an impartial judge to sum up:

One quite indiff'rent in the Cause,
My Character impartial draws:

'The Dean, if we believe Report,
'Was never ill receiv'd at Court:
'As for his Works in Verse and Prose,
'I own my self no Judge of those:
'Nor, can I tell what Criticks thought 'em;
'But, this I know, all People bought 'em;
'As with a moral View design'd
'To cure the Vices of Mankind:
'His Vein, ironically grave,
'Expos'd the Fool, and lash'd the Knave:
'To steal a Hint was never known,
'But what he writ was all his own.

'He never thought an Honour done him,
'Because a Duke was proud to own him:
'Would rather slip aside, and chuse
'To talk with Wits in dirty Shoes:
'Despis'd the Fools with Stars and Garters,
'So often seen caressing *Chartres*:
'He never courted Men in Station,

'*Nor Persons had in Admiration*;
'Of no Man's Greatness was afraid,
'Because he sought for no Man's Aid.
'Though trusted long in great Affairs,
'He gave himself no haughty Airs:
'Without regarding private Ends,
'Spent all his Credit for his Friends:
'And only chose the Wise and Good;
'No Flatt'rers; no Allies in Blood;
'But succour'd Virtue in Distress,
'And seldom fail'd of good Success;
'As Numbers in their Hearts must own,
'Who, but for him, had been unknown.

The Dispensary of **Sir Samuel Garth** (1661–1719) occupies an important place in the development of the mock-heroic poem. *Mack Flecknoe* had concerned itself only with a single episode. But Garth produced a full scale mock-heroic narrative in six cantos, which furnished the immediate model for *The Rape of the Lock*. The occasion of *The Dispensary* was the plan of the College of Physicians to establish in London a free dispensary for the poor. This scheme was opposed by the Apothecaries' Company. Since they themselves prescribed medicines at low cost, it interfered with their interests. Garth was himself a physician, and the imagery of the poem is largely drawn from the medical science of the day. The goddess of Discord arouses the apothecaries, and the two parties prepare to do battle, using syringes, urinals and the other tools of their trade. Hygeia, the goddess of Health, however, descends, and Celsus, one of the physicians, is sent to the Elysian Fields to consult the spirit of the great physician Harvey. The two contesting parties are instructed to refer their dispute to arbitration.

The Dispensary contains some striking passages of poetic description, such as that which describes Celsus's descent, through the bowels of the earth, to the Cave of Disease. Another takes the quack doctor Horoscope through the upper air on a journey to the Fortunate Isles:

With wonder he surveys the upper air,
And the gay gilded meteors sporting there.
How rising steams in the azure fluid blend,
Shoot through the ether in a trail of light;
How rising steams in the azure fluid blend,
Or fleet in clouds, or soft in showers descend;
Or if the stubborn rage of cold prevail,

In flakes they fly, or fall in moulded hail.
How honey-dews embalm the fragrant morn,
And the fair oak with luscious sweats adorn.
How heat and moisture mingle in a mass,
Or belch in thunder, or in lightening blaze.
Why nimble coruscations strike the eye,
And bold tornados bluster in the sky.
Why a prolific Aura upwards tends,
Ferments, and in a living shower descends.
How vapours hanging on the towering hills,
In breezes sigh, or weep in warbling rills:
Whence infant winds their tender pinions try,
And river-gods their thirsty urns supply.

The Augustan type of satire established by Dryden reaches its highest point of perfection in the work of **Alexander Pope** (1688–1744). Pope, whose ear for verse was well-nigh impeccable, refined the heroic couplet, emphasizing its antithetical nature, and often turning it into a self-contained epigrammatic unit. Almost all his important work is done in this form, and he very rarely admits the Drydenian licences of sometimes introducing a triplet or an Alexandrine. In his hands the couplet becomes an instrument of extraordinary delicacy and variety. He uses it for all purposes, ranging from the formally rhetorical to the conversational, and can also give it a lyrical or elegiac tone. He is perhaps only the inferior of Dryden in cogency and masculinity of thought, and in the capacity for welding his lines together to form a verse paragraph.

Although it is in the field of satire that Pope's greatest achievements were accomplished, it was mainly in the later part of his career that he 'stooped to truth, and moralized [his] song'.

Of the poems written by Pope in his twenties the *Pastorals* and *Windsor Forest* are devoted to formalized description of nature. *Eloisa to Abelard* and the *Elegy to the Memory of an Unfortunate Lady* are essays in pre-Romantic sensibility, while the *Essay on Criticism* discusses the principles central to Augustan poetry. This leaves only *The Rape of the Lock* in the category of satire, and it is rather to be considered as light raillery. The occasion of this poem was a quarrel between two of the families of Roman Catholic gentry in whose circle Pope moved. Lord Petrie (the Baron) surreptitiously cut a lock of hair from the head of Miss Arabella Fermor (Belinda). This might well have compromised her, and led to hard feelings. John Caryll, a friend of both families and of Pope's, suggested that the latter might heal the breach by making light of the incident. This he did in what may be considered the most formally perfect mock-heroic poem in all literature. It is a rococo fantasy, in which all the stock properties of traditional epic – the sacrifice, the heroic combats and so on – are given an equivalent in the artificial world of the toilet, the coffee table and the card party. The poem was first published in Addison's *Spectator*, and its tone of gentle mockery is generally Addisonian. Pope later added the machinery of the sylphs, though Addison was afraid that by so doing he would 'spoil a very pretty thing'. Addison's fears were unjustified, for this Rosicrucian mythology of aerial beings is perfectly fitted to the miniature scale of the poem:

> He summons strait his Denizens of air;
> The lucid squadrons round the sails repair:
> Soft o'er the shrouds aerial whispers breathe,
> That seem'd but Zephyrs to the train beneath.
> Some to the sun their insect-wings unfold,
> Waft on the breeze, or sink in clouds of gold;
> Transparent forms, too fine for mortal sight,
> Their fluid bodies half dissolv'd in light.
> Loose to the wind their airy garments flew,
> Thin glitt'ring textures of the filmy dew,
> Dipt in the richest tincture of the skies,
> Where light disports in ever-mingling dyes,
> While ev'ry beam new transient colours flings,
> Colours that change whene'er they wave their wings.

In the description of the Cave of Spleen (partly modelled on Garth's Cave of Disease) the imagery takes on a rather nightmarish, quasi-surrealistic quality. Spleen is the minor hell of neurosis which lies in wait for those who abandon good sense and good humour. It is this latter quality which it is the design of the poem to keep up, and its moral is to be found in the speech of Clarissa in Canto V:

> But since, alas! frail beauty must decay,
> Curl'd or uncurl'd, since Locks will turn to grey;
> Since painted, or not painted, all shall fade,
> And she who scorns a man, must die a maid;
> What then remains but well our pow'r to use,
> And keep good-humour still, whate'er we lose?
> And trust me, dear! good-humour can prevail,
> When airs, and flights, and screams, and scolding fail.
> Beauties in vain their pretty eyes may roll;
> Charms strike the sight, but merit wins the soul.

Pope's translation of Homer forms the turning point of his career. Not only did the hard labour involved in this task strengthen and mature his style, but the proceeds of the work made him financially independent. He was able to buy the lease of his villa at Twickenham, and there in country retirement, though within easy reach of London, he devoted himself to the composition and continual correction of his poems. Pope assumes the Horatian mask of the detached moralist and observer of life, who eschews power and public office, and stands above party. In fact, as a Roman Catholic, Pope was not eligible for public office, and since the death of Queen Anne his Tory friends were out of power with very little hope of regaining it. Power was in the hands of the Whigs under Sir Robert Walpole. Walpole gave the country the stability and economic prosperity it needed, but remained in office through systematic bribery and corruption and a fairly unscrupulous control of the press. Pope and his associates saw this as an ever-widening threat to all that they most valued. In the *Epilogue to the Satires* he paints a scarifying picture of contemporary England:

Vice is undone, if she forgets her Birth,
And stoops from Angels to the Dregs of Earth:
But 'tis the *Fall* degrades her to a Whore;
Let *Greatness* own her, and she's mean no more:
Her Birth, her Beauty, Crowds and Courts confess,
Chaste Matrons praise her, and grave Bishops bless:
In golden Chains the willing World she draws,
And hers the Gospel is, and hers the Laws:
Mounts the Tribunal, lifts her scarlet head,
And sees pale Virtue carted in her stead!
Lo! at the Wheels of her Triumphal Car,
Old *England's* Genius, rough with many a Scar,
Dragg'd in the Dust! his Arms hang idly round,
His Flag inverted trails along the ground!
Our Youth, all liv'ryed o'er with foreign Gold,
Before her dance; behind her crawl the Old!
See thronging Millions to the Pagod run,
And offer Country, Parent, Wife, or Son!
Hear her black Trumpet thro' the Land proclaim,
That 'Not to be corrupted is the Shame'.
In Soldier, Churchman, Patriot, Man in Pow'r,
'Tis Av'rice all, Ambition is no more!
See, all our Nobles begging to be Slaves!
See, all our Fools aspiring to be Knaves!

The Wit of Cheats, the Courage of a Whore,
Are what ten thousand envy and adore.
All, all look up, with reverential Awe,
On Crimes that scape, or triumph o'er the Law:
While Truth, Worth, Wisdom, daily they decry –
'Nothing is Sacred now but Villany'.

Together with the *Prologue to the Satires* (the *Epistle to Arbuthnot*) this poem constitutes Pope's apologia, in which he defends the right and duty of the satirist to attack vice and folly wherever he sees them. The Epilogue consists of two Dialogues; the Prologue of one in which Pope's interlocutor is Dr. John Arbuthnot, his personal physician, friend and literary associate. This is one of Pope's finest poems, and opens dramatically, as the poet represents himself as driven almost to distraction by the continual siege of bad writers who seek to pay court to him. The 'John' of the opening line is Pope's manservant:

Shut, shut the door, good John! fatigu'd I said,
Tie up the knocker, say I'm sick, I'm dead.
The Dog-star rages! nay 't is past a doubt,
All Bedlam, or Parnassus, is let out:
Fire in each eye, and papers in each hand,
They rave, recite, and madden round the land.
What walls can guard me, or what shade can hide?
They pierce my thickets, thro' my Grot they glide;
By land, by water, they renew the charge;
They stop the chariot, and they board the barge.
No place is sacred, not the Church is free;
Ev'n Sunday shines no Sabbath-day to me;
Then from the Mint walks forth the Man of rhyme,
Happy to catch me just at Dinner-time.

Pope goes on to describe his own career, and to declare his disinterestedness. He claims that his attacks on particular persons were always retaliations for slights upon himself, and that gossip has been too ready to identify his victims as individuals, when he himself intended only to portray general types. (Modern research has largely tended to vindicate Pope's character on both these points.) Nevertheless, he says, he will not fear to expose wickedness even among those in the highest positions of society:

P. Let *Sporus* tremble – A. What? that thing of silk,
Sporus, that mere white curd of Ass's milk?
Satire or sense, alas! can *Sporus* feel?
Who breaks a butterfly upon a wheel?

P. Yet let me flap this bug with gilded wings,
This painted child of dirt, that stinks and stings;
Whose buzz the witty and the fair annoys,
Yet wit ne'er tastes, and beauty ne'er enjoys:
So well-bred spaniels civilly delight
In mumbling of the game they dare not bite.
Eternal smiles his emptiness betray,
As shallow streams run dimpling all the way.
Whether in florid impotence he speaks,
And, as the prompter breathes, the puppet squeaks;
Or at the ear of *Eve*, familiar Toad,
Half froth, half venom, spits himself abroad,
In puns, or politics, or tales, or lies,
Or spite, or smut, or rhymes, or blasphemies.
His wit all see-saw, between *that* and *this*,
Now high, now low, now master up, now miss,
And he himself one vile Antithesis.
Amphibious thing! that acting either part
The trifling head or the corrupted heart,
Fop at the toilet, flatt'rer at the board,
Now trips a Lady, and now struts a Lord.
Eve's tempter thus the Rabbins have exprest,
A Cherub's face, a reptile all the rest;
Beauty that shocks you, parts that none will trust;
Wit that can creep, and pride that licks the dust.

This famous attack on Lord Hervey deserves careful scrutiny. Its poetic texture is extraordinarily complex. Images suggestive of sexual ambiguity, referring to Hervey's effeminateness, run through it, together with the images of unpleasant animals. These latter lead on to the figure of the toad at the ear of Eve. This refers to Hervey's collaboration with Lady Mary Wortley Montagu in a literary attack on Pope, and perhaps to his confidential relationship with Queen Caroline. But it also alludes to the passage in *Paradise Lost* where Satan is discovered in the form of a toad whispering a seductive dream into Eve's ear while she sleeps. This prepares the way for the image of the serpent with a woman's face in which both trains of imagery meet. What first appeared merely as a tiresome insect, not worth crushing, is now seen as something satanic, spreading corruption at the very heart of society. This is clinched in the final image of pride that licks the dust – the punishment inflicted on the serpent after the Fall.

The satires which this Prologue and Epilogue frame, are the *Imitations of Horace*. The imitation had become a widespread and characteristic Augustan mode. Earlier examples are to be found in the works of Oldham and Rochester. It is a free form of translation, in which the poet takes an ancient poem as his starting point, but alters or expands it to make it applicable to the circumstances of his own age. Thus in Pope's satires, Horace's allusions to contemporary Roman personalities are replaced by equivalents in eighteenth-century London. Where Horace cites examples from ancient Roman history, parallel instances from English history are given. The procedure was made possible by the fact that there was a real analogy between the society of Augustan Rome and that of eighteenth-century England. In both periods a time of stability had succeeded one of instability and civil strife, and in both a new, principally commercial aristocracy (the Roman *equites*, the Whig magnates) had gained the ascendancy. Traditional moral and social standards were consequently felt to be declining. Both early imperial Rome and eighteenth-century London were urban societies – large, but not so large that the members of the cultured élite should not be all in touch with one another; and in both cases there was a solid rural background.

Of the *Imitations of Horace* themselves the most interesting and the most daring is the *Epistle to Augustus*, addressed by Pope to George II. The Emperor Augustus had been, through his minister Maecenas, an enlightened patron of letters. The same could hardly be said of George II, and, indeed, after the accession of the Hanoverian dynasty, the English court lost, and can scarcely be said ever to have regained, that close connection with the best literary culture of the age which it possessed in Tudor and Stuart times. Pope therefore transposes Horace's poem into a mood of bitter irony. In recommending the patronage of poetry to Augustus, Horace had made a plea for the new and more polished writers of his own generation as against the older writers of the Roman Republic whom some affected to prefer. In Pope's satire this becomes a criticism of the growing antiquarian interest in earlier English writers:

> Authors, like Coins, grow dear as they grow old;
> It is the rust we value, not the gold.
> Chaucer's worst ribaldry is learn'd by rote,
> And beastly Skelton Heads of Houses quote:
> One likes no language but the Faery Queen;
> A Scot will fight for Christ's Kirk o' the Green;
> And each true Briton is to Ben so civil,
> He swears the Muses met him at the Devil.

The Devil Tavern in Fleet Street was one frequented by Ben Jonson. Pope is hardly fair to the merits of the fifteenth-century Scottish poem *Christ's Kirk o' the Green*, and certainly unjust to Skelton. But the point he is making has some validity, and is also made in the *Dunciad*.

The *Epistle to Augustus* ends with an audaciously inverted panegyric:

> Oh! could I mount on the Maeonian wing,
> Your Arms, your Actions, your Repose to sing!
> What seas you travers'd! and what fields you fought!
> Your Country's Peace, how oft, how dearly bought!
> How barb'rous rage subsided at your word,
> And Nations wonder'd while they dropp'd the sword!
> How, when you nodded, o'er the land and deep,
> Peace stole her wing, and wrapt the world in sleep;
> Till Earth's extremes your mediation own,
> And Asia's Tyrants tremble at your Throne –
> But Verse alas! your Majesty disdains;
> And I'm not us'd to Panegyric strains:
> The Zeal of Fools offends at any time,
> But most of all, the Zeal of Fools in ryme.
> Besides, a fate attends on all I write,
> That when I aim at praise, they say I bite.
> A Vile Encomium doubly ridicules;
> There's nothing blackens like the ink of fools;
> If true, a woful likeness, and if lyes,
> 'Praise undeserv'd is scandal in disguise:
> Well may he blush, who gives it, or receives;
> And when I flatter, let my dirty leaves
> (Like Journals, Odes, and such forgotten things
> As Eusden, Philips, Settle, writ of Kings)
> Cloath spice, line trunks, or flutt'ring in a row,
> Befringe the rails of Bedlam and Sohoe.

Pope's *Moral Essays* (otherwise called *Ethick Epistles*) were originally intended to form, together with the *Essay on Man*, a single extended work. This was to be a series of Horatian epistles, in which man was to be discussed, first in relation to his place in nature, and then in his aesthetic, economic and political aspects. The purpose of the *Moral Essays* then is didactic and philosophical, and only incidentally satiric. They do, however, contain some of Pope's most notable passages in this vein. Among these is the famous picture of Timon's Villa in the fourth of the *Moral Essays* Book II. The Villa is an example both of false taste and of the misuse of riches. Its owner is evidently a member of the new Whig aristocracy. Contemporary gossip identified him with the Duke of Chandos, whose country seat was Canons, near London. But Pope claimed, probably rightly, that it was a composite picture:

> At Timon's Villa let us pass a day,
> Where all cry out, 'What sums are thrown away!'
> So proud, so grand; of that stupendous air,
> Soft and Agreeable come never there.
> Greatness, with Timon, dwells in such a draught
> As brings all Brobdignag before your thought.
> To compass this, his building is a Town,
> His pond an Ocean, his parterre a Down:
> Who but must laugh, the Master when he sees,
> A puny insect, shiv'ring at a breeze!
> Lo, what huge heaps of littleness around!
> The whole, a labour'd Quarry above ground;
> Two Cupids squirt before; a Lake behind
> Improves the keenness of the Northern wind.
> His Gardens next your admiration call,
> On ev'ry side you look, behold the Wall!
> No pleasing Intricacies intervene,
> No artful wildness to perplex the scene;
> Grove nods at grove, each Alley has a brother,
> And half the platform just reflects the other.
> The suff'ring eye inverted Nature sees,
> Trees cut to Statues, Statues thick as trees;
> With here a Fountain, never to be play'd;
> And there a Summer-house, that knows no shade;
> Here Amphitrite sails thro' myrtle bow'rs;
> There Gladiators fight, or die in flow'rs;
> Un-watered see the drooping sea-horse mourn,
> And swallows roost in Nilus' dusty Urn.

This house and its formal gardens are in the extravagant rococco taste. Sir Richard Boyle, to whom the poem is addressed, was a principal advocate in England of the more restrained Palladian style. Pope himself contributed to Steele's *Guardian* an essay on landscape gardens. The principle of the English landscape garden is the Popean one of 'Nature methodized'. It blends with the surrounding landscape. But that of Timon's Villa is wholly cut off from nature, and contrary to it.

Pope's second mock-heroic poem, *The Dunciad*, is quite different in purpose and scope from *The Rape of the Lock*. In its original form, it is not only an attack on Lewis Theobald, but also on the whole tribe of party and commercial hack writers associated with Grub Street. It is a mistake to regard Pope as motivated only by a desire for personal revenge. It is true that Theobald had offended Pope by criticizing adversely the latter's edition of Shakespeare; it is also true that, from the point of view of textual scholarship, Theobald was Pope's superior. But this quarrel, like that with Richard Bentley, involved deeper issues. It is that which still exists between the merely verbal critic and scholar and those who attempt a broader and more humane approach to literature. This humane tradition Pope saw as also threatened by the commercialization and prostitution of writing, and its subordination to party interests, which the rise of the bookseller-publishers and Walpole's political régime seemed to him to be bringing about. The Goddess of Dulness who presides over *The Dunciad* is the daughter of Chaos and Old Night. The poem is full of Miltonic echoes. The Goddess, through her children, the Dunces, seeks to restore the rule of those primal powers which were before the creation of the ordered cosmos. It was with these that, in Milton's poem, Satan leagued himself before his assault on the newly-created world. For Pope, bad writing of any kind is a moral as well as an aesthetic offence. By corrupting language it strikes at the roots of human reason and communication, and hence at civilization itself. The rise of the Dunces threatens a second Dark Age, comparable to that which succeeded the fall of the Roman Empire:

> How little, mark! that portion of the ball,
> Where, faint at best, the beams of Science fall:
> Soon as they dawn, from Hyperborean skies
> Embody'd dark, what clouds of Vandals rise!
> Lo! where Mæotis sleeps, and hardly flows
> The freezing Tanais thro' a waste of snows,
> The North by myriads pours her mighty sons,
> Great nurse of Goths, of Alans, and of Huns!
> See Alaric's stern port! the martial frame
> Of Genseric! and Attila's dread name!
> See the bold Ostrogoths on Latium fall;
> See the fierce Visigoths on Spain and Gaul!
> See, where the morning gilds the palmy shore
> (The soil that arts and infant letters bore)
> His conqu'ring tribes th'Arabian prophet draws,
> And saving Ignorance enthrones by Laws.
> See Christians, Jews, one heavy sabbath keep,
> And all the western world believe and sleep.

In the final version of *The Dunciad*, Pope not only added the Fourth Book which is almost a distinct poem in its own right, but also deposed Theobald from his position as ruler of the realm of Dulness in favour of Colley Cibber. Cibber had offended Pope by caricaturing him on the stage; he was a rather amiable character, and by no means an incompetent dramatist. Pope had praised his *Careless Husband* in the *Epistle to Augustus*. But it was really his appointment as Poet Laureate which singled him out for the position of King of the Dunces. His official odes are laughably bad, and he owed the post wholly to his sound Whiggish opinions.

In the Fourth Book of *The Dunciad* the scope of Pope's satire is extended. The false values of Grub Street are seen as invading the fashionable world, the universities, the Inns of Court, and finally the entire nation. Other objects of Pope's scorn include virtuosi, antiquarians and amateur naturalists. Like the inhabitants of Swift's Laputa they devote their time to abstruse and trivial researches instead of to humane and practical learning –

> The mind in metaphysics at a loss
> May wander in a wilderness of moss.

The Fourth Book opens with a striking image suggestive of a drawing by Hogarth:

> Yet, yet a moment, one dim Ray of Light
> Indulge, dread Chaos, and eternal Night!
> Of darkness visible so much be lent,
> As half to shew, half veil, the deep Intent.
> Ye Pow'rs! whose Mysteries restor'd I sing,
> To whom Time bears me on his rapid wing,
> Suspend awhile your Force inertly strong,
> Then take at once the Poet and the Song.
> Now flam'd the Dog-star's unpropitious ray,
> Smote ev'ry Brain, and wither'd ev'ry Bay;
> Sick was the Sun, the Owl forsook his bow'r,
> The moon-struck Prophet felt the madding hour:
> Then rose the Seed of Chaos, and of Night,
> To blot out Order, and extinguish Light,
> Of dull and venal a new World to mould,
> And bring Saturnian days of Lead and Gold.
> She mounts the Throne: her head a Cloud conceal'd
> In broad Effulgence all below reveal'd;
> ('T is thus aspiring Dulness ever shines)
> Soft on her lap her Laureate son reclines.

Beneath her footstool, *Science* groans in Chains,
And Wit dreads Exile, Penalties, and Pains.
There foam'd rebellious *Logic*, gagg'd and bound,
There, stript, fair *Rhet'ric* languished on the ground;
His blunted Arms by *Sophistry* are borne,
And shameless *Billingsgate* her Robes adorn.
Morality, by her false guardians drawn,
Chicane in Furs, and *Casuistry* in Lawn,
Gasps, as they straiten at each end the cord,
And dies, when Dulness gives her Page the word.

The final triumph of Dulness is prophesied in the famous concluding passage. In this we see the whole traditional hierarchy of the Arts and Sciences overthrown. Pope may not seriously have envisaged such a total breakdown, but he did see the resurgence of barbarism as a real threat; it is recorded that he never read this passage without tears coming into his eyes:

She comes! she comes! the sable Throne behold
Of *Night* Primæval and of *Chaos* old!
Before her, *Fancy's* gilded clouds decay,
And all its varying Rain-bows die away.
Wit shoots in vain its momentary fires,
The meteor drops, and in a flash expires.
As one by one, at dread Medea's strain,
The sick'ning stars fade off th'ethereal plain;
As Argus' eyes by Hermes' wand oppress,
Clos'd one by one to everlasting rest;
Thus at her felt approach, and secret might,
Art after *Art* goes out, and all is Night.
See skulking *Truth* to her old cavern fled,
Mountains of Casuistry heap'd o'er her head!
Philosophy, that lean'd on Heav'n before,
Shrinks to her second cause, and is no more.
Physic of *Metaphysic* begs defence,
And *Metaphysic* calls for aid on *Sense*!
See *Mystery* to *Mathematics* fly!
In vain! they gaze, turn giddy, rave, and die.
Religion, blushing, veils her sacred fires,
And unawares *Morality* expires.
Nor *public* Flame, nor *private*, dares to shine;
Nor *human* Spark is left, nor Glimpse *divine*!
Lo! thy dread Empire, CHAOS! is restor'd;

Light dies before thy uncreating word:
Thy hand, great Anarch! lets the curtain fall
And universal Darkness buries All.

Edward Young (1683–1765) is chiefly known as the author of the *Night Thoughts*. This gloomy religious and didactic poem enjoyed a European reputation, but is now largely unreadable. There is some wit in it, but it does not sort very well with the stiff and pompous blank verse. Young's satires, in *The Love of Fame, The Universal Passion*, are much livelier, and, at least in the opinion of the present writer, are his best work. Young admired Pope, but takes a gentler tone, which he defends in his Preface:

Laughing at the misconduct of the world will, in a great measure, ease us of any more disagreeable passion about it. One passion is more effectually driven out by another than by reason, whatever some may teach. For to reason we owe our passions; had we not reason, we should not be offended at what we find amiss: and the cause seems not to be the natural cure of any effect.

Moreover, laughing satire bids the fairest for success. The world is too proud to be fond of a serious tutor; and when an author is in a passion, the laugh, generally, as in conversation, turns against him. This kind of satire only has any delicacy in it. Of this delicacy Horace is the best master: he appears in good humour while he censures; and therefore his censure has the more weight, as supposed to proceed from judgement, not from passion. Juvenal is ever in a passion: he has little valuable but his eloquence and morality; the last of which I have had in my eye, but rather for emulation than imitation, through my whole work.

Young adds an innovation by giving a unity to his series of satires. They are all made to refer to the universal passion of the title. In this he departs from the practice of his predecessors. Since the etymology of the word 'satire' implied a miscellany, it was not generally held to require unity of subject matter. From the love of fame the author admits that he himself is not exempt:

O thou myself! abroad our counsels roam,
And, like ill husbands, take no care at home.
Thou, too, art wounded with the common dart,
And Love of Fame lies throbbing at thy heart;
And what wise means to gain it hast thou chose?
Know, Fame and Fortune both are made of prose.
Is thy ambition sweating for a rhyme,
Thou unambitious fool, at this late time?
While I a moment name, a moment's past;
I'm nearer death in this verse than the last:

What, then, is to be done? Be wise with speed;
A fool at forty is a fool indeed.
And what so foolish as the chase of Fame?
How vain the prize! how impotent our aim!
For what are men who grasp at praise sublime,
But bubbles on the rapid stream of time,
That rise and fall, that swell and are no more,
Born and forgot, ten thousand in a hour?

Young's tone is that of the fashionable preacher – a position, which as a clergyman, he would have liked to have attained. He is, perhaps, at his best in the two satires which he devotes to the foibles of women. These contain a series of character sketches which are worth comparing with those of Pope in his *Essay on the Characters of Women*. This is Young's portrait of a frivolous religious *dévote*:

Lavinia is polite, but not profane;
To church as constant as to Drury-Lane.
She decently, in form, pays Heaven its due,
And makes a civil visit to her pew.
Her lifted fan, to give a solemn air,
Conceals her face, which passes for a prayer:
Curtsies to curtsies, then, with grace succeed;
Not one the fair omits, but at the Creed.
Or if she joins the service, 't is to speak;
Through dreadful silence the pent heart might break;
Untaught to bear it, women talk away
To God himself, and fondly think they pray.
But sweet their accent, and their air refined;
For they're before their Maker – and mankind.
When ladies once are proud of praying well,
Satan himself will toll the parish bell.

The macabre tone, characteristic of the *Night Thoughts*, sometimes invades Young's satire, though not ineffectively:

'*But adoration*? Give *me* something more',
Cries Lyce, on the borders of threescore.
Nought treads so silent as the foot of Time;
Hence we mistake our autumn for our prime.
'T is greatly wise to know, before we're told,
The melancholy news, that we grow old.
Autumnal Lyce carries in her face
Memento mori to each public place.

O how your beating breast a mistress warms
Who looks through spectacles to see your charms!
While rival undertakers hover round,
And with his spade the sexton marks the ground,
Intent not on her own, but others' doom,
She plans new conquests, and defrauds the tomb.
In vain the cock has summon'd sprites away,
She walks at noon, and blasts the bloom of day.
Gay rainbow silks her mellow charms infold,
And nought of Lyce but *herself* is old.
Her grizzled locks assume a smirking grace,
And Art has levell'd her deep-furrow'd face.
Her strange demand no mortal can approve;
We'll ask her blessing, but can't ask her love.
She grants, indeed, a lady *may* decline
(All ladies but herself) at ninety-nine!

6

The Eighteenth Century: II

The two principal poems of **Samuel Johnson** (1709–84), *London* and *The Vanity of Human Wishes*, are both imitations of Juvenal, being based on the latter's third and tenth satires respectively. But Johnson's melancholy and courageous view of human life, and his peculiar greatness, are stamped on every line of them. Johnson's handling of the couplet derives from that of Pope, but his lines have a grave music and a weight of gnomic utterance which is his own. *London* deals with the conventional theme of the inconveniences of city life and the advantages of country retirement:

> For who would leave, unbrib'd, Hibernia's Land,
> Or change the Rocks of *Scotland* for the *Strand*?
> There none are swept by sudden Fate away,
> But all whom Hunger spares, with Age decay:
> Here Malice, Rapine, Accident, conspire,
> And now a Rabble rages, now a Fire;
> Their Ambush here relentless Ruffians lay,
> And here the fell Attorney prowls for Prey;
> Here falling Houses thunder on your Head,
> And here a female Atheist talks you dead.

These sentiments may not seem quite in accord with those which Johnson was apt to express in conversation – about Scotland for instance, or that he who is tired of London is tired of life. But he writes with deep personal feeling, and out of experience, when he comes to speak of the miseries of poverty:

> Has Heaven reserv'd, in Pity to the Poor,
> No pathless Waste, or undiscover'd Shore?
> No secret Island in the boundless Main?
> No peaceful Desart yet unclaim'd by SPAIN?
> Quick let us rise, the happy Seats explore,
> And bear Oppression's Insolence no more.
> This mournful Truth is ev'ry where confest,
> SLOW RISES WORTH, BY POVERTY DEPREST:
> But here more slow, where all are Slaves to Gold,
> Where looks are Merchandise, and Smiles are sold,

Where won by Bribes, by Flatteries implor'd,
The Groom retails the Favours of his Lord.

The Vanity of Human Wishes is the finer of the two poems. Perhaps the most memorable passage is that which deals with Charles of Sweden. His spectacular military career reached its climax in his invasion of Russia, but he died by a chance shot while laying siege to a Norwegian fortress. This also illustrates very well the principle of imitation. The original passage in Juvenal cited the career of Hannibal, for whom Johnson thus successfully finds a modern parallel:

Peace courts his Hand, but spreads her Charms in vain;
'Think Nothing gain'd, he cries, till nought remain,
On *Moscow's* Walls till *Gothic* Standards fly,
And all is Mine beneath the Polar Sky.'
The March begins in Military State,
And Nations on his Eye suspended wait;
Stern Famine guards the solitary Coast,
And Winter barricades the Realms of Frost;
He comes, nor Want nor Cold his Course delay; –
Hide, blushing Glory, hide *Pultowa's* Day:
The vanquish'd Hero leaves his broken Bands,
And shews his Miseries in distant lands;
Condemn'd a needy Supplicant to wait,
While Ladies interpose, and Slaves debate.
But did not Chance at length her Error mend?
Did no subverted Empire mark his End?
Did rival Monarchs give the fatal Wound?
Or hostile Millions press him to the Ground?
His Fall was destin'd to a barren Strand,
A petty Fortress, and a dubious Hand;
He left the Name, at which the World grew pale,
To point a Moral, or adorn a Tale.

At the close of the poem, Johnson substitutes a definitely Christian moral for the pagan stoicism of Juvenal:

Where then shall Hope and Fear their Objects find?
Must dull Suspence corrupt the stagnant Mind?
Must helpless Man, in Ignorance sedate,
Swim darkling down the Current of his Fate?
Must no Dislike alarm, no Wishes rise,
No Cries attempt the Mercies of the Skies?
Enquirer, cease, Petitions yet remain,

Which Heav'n may hear, nor deem Religion vain.
Still raise for Good the supplicating Voice,
But leave to Heav'n the Measure and the Choice.
Safe in his Pow'r, whose Eyes discern afar
The secret Ambush of a specious Pray'r.
Implore his Aid, in his Decisions rest,
Secure whate'er he gives, he gives the best.
Yet with the sense of sacred Presence prest,
When strong Devotion fills thy glowing Breast,
Pour forth thy Fervours for a healthful Mind,
Obedient Passions, and a Will resign'd;
For Love, which scarce collective Man can fill;
For Patience sov'reign o'er transmuted Ill;
For Faith, that panting for a happier Seat,
Thinks Death kind Nature's Signal of Retreat:
These Goods for Man the Laws of Heav'n ordain,
These Goods he grants, who grants the Pow'r to gain;
With these celestial Wisdom calms the Mind,
And makes the Happiness she does not find.

Johnson is really the last great representative of the Augustan classical style as it had been perfected by Pope. The poetic values which he championed were, during his lifetime, being continually challenged by an incipient Romanticism. Even satire, the most characteristic Augustan form, did not remain unaffected by the new spirit. The satirists whom we shall deal with in the remainder of this chapter all either modified the vehicle of the closed heroic couplet, or abandoned it altogether. Three of them were also strongly radical in their political standpoint. But even the evangelicalism of Cowper is in its own way as much a challenge to the High Church and Tory values represented by Johnson.

Charles Churchill (1731–64) was an angry young man, who 'blazed' (as Byron was to say) 'the comet of a season', and earned himself the title of the British Juvenal. Although his poems were reprinted in the nineteenth and the twentieth centuries, they have, on the whole, been neglected since his death. It is generally said that they are too closely linked to the political and other events of his own day; but the same is, after all, also true of Dryden, and indeed of most of the satirists we have been considering. We must conclude, therefore, that Churchill lacked the power to give to his subject matter universal and enduring significance. Nevertheless, both his life and writings are interesting, and deserve more than cursory study. He became a clergyman, but was obliged to resign his orders, and was a close friend and associate of John

Wilkes, that courageous, but personally dissolute, champion of liberty. He died at the early age of thirty-three, at Boulogne, having fled to the Continent to escape arrest and to join Wilkes. His body was later removed to Dover, and Byron visited his grave there before leaving England for the last time:

> I stood beside the grave of him who blazed
>   The comet of a season, and I saw
> The humblest of all sepulchres, and gazed
>   With not the less of sorrow and of awe
> On that neglected turf and quiet stone,
> With name no clearer than the names unknown,
> Which lay unread around it; and I ask'd
>   The Gardener of that ground, why it might be
> That for this plant strangers his memory task'd,
>   Through the thick deaths of half a century?

Byron evidently saw in Churchill a literary forerunner and a type of his own destiny. In this he was not mistaken. Churchill, like Byron, wrote hastily and often carelessly. Though he continued to employ the heroic couplet, he departed from the rigid antithetical form of it. His aim seems to have been to return to the Drydenesque model, using a certain freedom of *enjambement*, and making the paragraph, rather than the single couplet, the unit. He lacks, however, Dryden's control in building up a paragraph, and the effect is often rather breathless. But what differentiates Churchill's work from classical Augustan satire most of all is his abandonment of the mask of detached objectivity, and the frank intrusion of his own strong and rather disordered personality.

Churchill began his poetical career with a satire on the contemporary theatre, *The Rosciad*. This poem, which discusses the characters and claims of the actors of the day, throws an interesting sidelight on the eighteenth-century stage. But he soon turned to political satire. *The Prophecy of Famine* expresses the widespread resentment against the Scots, and especially those who came to make a career in England, which existed under Lord Bute's administration. It is in the form of a mock pastoral, and paints a gloomy picture of Scotland itself:

> Far as the eye could reach, no tree was seen,
> Earth, clad in russet, scorn'd the lively green.
> The plague of Locusts they secure defy,
> For in three hours a grasshopper must die.
> No living thing, whate'er its food, feasts there,

But the Cameleon, who can feast on air.
No birds, except as birds of passage, flew,
No bee was known to hum, no dove to coo.
No streams as amber smooth, as amber clear,
Were seen to glide, or heard to warble here.
Rebellion's spring, which through the country ran,
Furnish'd, with bitter draughts, the steady clan.
No flowers embalm'd the air, but one white rose,
Which, on the tenth of June, by instinct blows,
By instinct blows at morn, and, when the shades
Of drizly eve prevail, by instinct fades.

The white rose is, of course, the emblem of the Jacobites, and was worn by them on the tenth of June, the Young Pretender's birthday. Churchill mounts a withering attack on the whole house of Stuart in *Gotham*, perhaps the best of his satires. In this poem he fancies himself made king of the imaginary land of Gotham, and then launches into a general satire on English kings, and a discussion of what a king ought to be. The following is part of his character of James I:

Lies were his Play-things, Parliaments his sport;
Book-worms and Catamites engross'd the Court;
Vain of the Scholar, like all SCOTSMEN since,
The *Pedant* Scholar, he forgot the Prince,
And, having with some trifles stor'd his brain,
Ne'er learn'd, or wish'd to learn the arts to reign.
Enough he knew, to make him vain and proud,
Mock'd by the wise, the wonder of the crowd;
False Friend, false Son, false Father, and false King,
False Wit, false Statesman, and false ev'ry thing,
When He should act, he idly chose to prate,
And pamphlets wrote, when he should save the State.

In a later passage, where Churchill speaks of his early devotion to poetry, the tone becomes almost Romantic:

When dreary NIGHT, with MORPHEUS in her train,
Led on by SILENCE to resume her reign,
With Darkness covering, as with a robe,
This scene of Levity, blank'd half the globe,
How oft', enchanted with your heav'nly strains,
Which stole me from myself, which in soft chains
Of Musick bound my soul, how oft' have I,
Sounds more than human floating thro' the Sky,

Attentive sat, whilst NIGHT, against her Will,
Transported with the harmony, stood still!
How oft' in raptures, which Man scarce could bear,
Have I, when gone, still thought the Muses there;
Still heard their Musick, and, as mute as death,
Sat all attention, drew in ev'ry Breath,
Lest, breathing all too rudely, I should wound,
And marr that magic excellence of sound:
Then, Sense returning with return of Day,
Have chid the Night, which fled so fast away.

The Ghost is a satire in octosyllabic couplets in the manner of Butler. Its central subject is the so-called cock-laying ghost – an alleged supernatural phenomenon which eventually turned out to be due to fraud. But Churchill wanders from his main theme, human credulity and superstition, to display his personal opinions and some out-of-the-way learning. George Gilfillan, Churchill's nineteenth-century editor, perceptively compares the form of this poem to *Tristram Shandy* and to *Don Juan*. Among those who investigated the cock-laying ghost was Johnson, and Churchill includes the following unsympathetic portrait of him:

POMPOSO (insolent and loud,)
Vain idol of a *scribbling* crowd,
Whose very name inspires an awe,
Whose ev'ry word is Sense and Law,
For what his Greatness hath decreed,
Like Laws of PERSIA and of MEDE,
Sacred thro' all the realm of *Wit*,
Must never of Repeal admit;
Who, cursing flatt'ry, is the tool
Of ev'ry fawning flatt'ring fool;
Who Wit with jealous eye surveys,
And sickens at another's praise;
Who, proudly seiz'd of *Learning*'s throne,
Now damns all Learning but his own;
Who scorns those common wares to trade in,
Reas'ning, *Convincing*, and *Persuading*,
But makes each Sentence current pass
With *Puppy*, *Coxcomb*, *Scoundrel*, *Ass*;
For 'tis with *him* a certain rule,
The Folly's prov'd when he calls Fool;
Who, to increase his native strength,
Draws words, six syllables in length,

With which, assisted with a frown
By way of Club, he knocks us down.

Churchill's dislike of Johnson was reciprocated. The Doctor described the younger poet as 'a prolific blockhead', 'a huge and infertile crab-tree'. Churchill was notable for his physical bulk, and Hogarth caricatured him as a bear in clerical bands.

Churchill's remaining poems may be considered as Juvenalian satires. The closest in tone to the Latin master is *The Times*. This is a very outspoken attack on the vices of contemporary society, especially the alleged prevalence of homosexuality. The following passage, from near the beginning of the poem, will serve to illustrate the most striking characteristic of Churchill's style – his breathless, headlong rhetoric:

Time was, ere Temperance had fled the realm,
Ere Luxury sat guttling at the helm
From meal to meal, without one moment's space
Reserv'd for business, or allow'd for grace;
Ere Vanity had so far conquer'd Sense
To make us all wild rivals in expence,
To make one Fool strive to outvye another,
And ev'ry coxcomb dress against his brother;
Ere banish'd Industry had left our shores,
And Labour was by Pride kick'd out of doors;
Ere Idleness prevail'd sole Queen in Courts,
Or only yielded to a rage for sports;
Ere each weak mind was with externals caught,
And Dissipation held the place of Thought;
Ere gambling lords so far in vice were gone
To cog the die, and bid the Sun look on;
Ere a great Nation, not less just than free,
Was made a beggar by Œconomy;
Ere rugged Honesty was out of vogue,
Ere Fashion stamp'd her sanction on the rogue;
Time was, that Men had conscience, that they made
Scruples to owe, what never could be paid.

But, as we have already said, what is most interesting in Churchill is the not infrequent appearance of a personal and autobiographical note, which contrasts with the tone of Olympian detachment generally adopted by the earlier Augustan satirists. This autobiographical element is to be found in his last poem, *The Journey*, left unfinished at his death, and in the following passage from *The Candidate*. Here Churchill writes his own epitaph, and seems to anticipate, as it were prophetically, Byron's visit to his grave which we have already mentioned:

> Let none of Those, whom I despise tho' great,
> Pretending Friendship to give malice weight,
> Publish my life; let no false, sneaking peer
> (Some such there are) to win the public ear,
> Hand me to shame with some vile anecdote,
> Nor soul-gall'd Bishop damn me with a note.
> Let one poor sprig of Bay around my head
> Bloom whilst I live, and point me out when dead;
> Let It (may Heav'n indulgent grant that pray'r)
> Be planted on my grave, nor wither there;
> And when, on travel bound, some riming guest
> Roams thro' the Church-yard, whilst his Dinner's dress'd,
> Let It hold up this Comment to his eyes;
> Life to the last enjoy'd, *here* Churchill lies;
> Whilst (O, what joy that pleasing flatt'ry gives)
> Reading my works, he cries – *here* Churchill lives.

It can hardly be said that Churchill's poetry has lived, except for a few familiar quotations. But the neglect into which his work has fallen is not wholly justified. He shows considerable vigour and originality, and had his life not been cut short he might have developed into a major poet.

A second Radical satirist is **John Wolcot** (Peter Pindar) (1738–1819). His pseudonym indicates his chosen form, a burlesque version of the free Pindaric ode. He did not, however, confine himself to this. His mock-heroic poem, *The Lousiad*, is in heroic couplets. It presents an amusing picture of the stuffy and philistine court of George III and Queen Charlotte. The King, while dining, finds a louse on his plate, and orders all his cooks to be shaved. They are indignant at the idea, and threaten revolt. The louse, like Belinda's lock, is translated to heaven where it becomes a star and is discovered by Herschel, the Astronomer Royal. Herschel did, in fact discover Uranus, and named it Georgium Sidus in honour of the King.

The following is from Wolcot's *Birthday Ode* on the visit of the King and Queen to Whitbread's brewery:

> Now boasting WHITBREAD serious did declare,
> To make the Majesty of England stare,
> That he had butts enough, he knew,
> Plac'd side by side, to reach along to Kew:
> On which the King with wonder swiftly cry'd,

'What, if they reach to Kew then, side by side,
'What would they do, what, what, plac'd end to end?'
To whom, with knitted calculating brow,
The Man of Beer most solemnly did vow,
Almost to Windsor that they would extend;
On which the King, with wond'ring mien,
Repeated it unto the wond'ring Queen:
On which, quick turning round his halter'd head,
The Brewer's horse, with face astonish'd, neigh'd;
The Brewer's dog too pour'd a note of thunder,
Rattled his chain, and wagg'd his tail for wonder.

Wolcot is a caricaturist; we might compare his work to that of the artist James Gillray, his contemporary. But in Wolcot's work satire really abandons its pretensions to being a serious poetic form, and falls to the sphere of light and burlesque verse. To this position it was to be increasingly relegated during the following century. Much the same may be said of another satirist of the late eighteenth century, **Christopher Anstey** (1724–1805). His *New Bath Guide* describes the adventures of the Blunderhead Family in fashionable Bath. It is in the form of imaginary letters in anapaestic verse. These letters may be compared with those of the Bramble Family in Smollett's *Humphry Clinker*.

The gentle and inoffensive **William Cowper** (1731–1800) possessed little or none of that capacity for *saeva indignatio* which we might take to be an essential constituent of the satirist's character. His satires are Horatian in manner, and are a good-humoured commentary on life as he sees it. Their strong tone of evangelical piety renders them a little prim, and at times even lurid, when Cowper's conviction of the damnation which awaits the worldly and the unbeliever comes to the fore. Their tone owes something to Young's satires; but technically Cowper is, in his quiet way, an innovator. Though he admired Pope, he saw clearly that Pope's balanced and antithetical use of the couplet had become, in the hands of later and lesser poets, trite and mechanical:

Then Pope, as harmony itself exact,
In verse well-disciplined, complete, compact,
Gave virtue and morality a grace
That, quite eclipsing pleasure's painted face,
Levied a tax of wonder and applause,
Even on the fools that trampled on their laws.
But he (his musical finesse was such,
So nice his ear, so delicate his touch)

Made poetry a mere mechanic art,
And every warbler has his tune by heart.
Nature imparting her satiric gift,
Her serious mirth, to Arbuthnot and Swift,
With droll sobriety they raised a smile
At folly's cost, themselves unmoved the while.
That constellation set, the world in vain
Must hope to look upon their like again.

Cowper himself aims at a more informal, conversational style. Furthermore, as an Evangelical, he believes that the heart as well as the head must be appealed to. With these ends in view, he abandons the pointed use of antithesis, and also treats the couplet much more freely. His use of *enjambement* owes something to the example of Churchill. Churchill had been his schoolfellow at Westminister, and Cowper pays the following tribute to his talents:

Churchill, himself unconscious of his powers,
In penury consumed his idle hours,
And, like a scattered seed at random sown,
Was left to spring by vigour of his own.
Lifted at length, by dignity of thought
And dint of genius, to an affluent lot,
He laid his head in luxury's soft lap,
And took too often there his easy nap.
If brighter beams than all he threw not forth,
'Twas negligence in him, not want of worth.
Surly and slovenly, and bold and coarse,
Too proud for art, and trusting in mere force,
Spendthrift alike of money and of wit,
Always at speed, and never drawing bit,
He struck the lyre in such a careless mood,
And so disdained the rules he understood,
The laurel seemed to wait on his command,
He snatched it rudely from the Muses' hand.

As a moralist Cowper is less convincing when he deals with the vices of the great world, of which in his retirement he could know nothing at first hand, than when he observes the foibles of the provincial scene around him. The following is still perhaps relevant to English conversational habits:

The circle formed, we sit in silent state,
Like figures drawn upon a dial-plate;

'Yes, Ma'am', and 'No, Ma'am', uttered softly, show
Every five minutes how the minutes go;
Each individual, suffering a constraint
Poetry may, but colours cannot paint,
As if in close committee on the sky,
Reports it hot or cold, or wet or dry;
And finds a changing clime a happy source
Of wise reflection, and well-timed discourse.
We next inquire, but softly and by stealth,
Like conservators of the public health,
Of epidemic throats, if such there are,
And coughs, and rheums, and phthisic, and catarrh.
That theme exhausted, a wide chasm ensues,
Filled up at last with interesting news,
Who danced with whom, and who are like to wed,
And who is hanged, and who is brought to bed;
But fear to call a more important cause,
As if 'twere treason against English laws.
The visit paid, with ecstasy we come,
As from a seven years' transportation, home.

As we have already indicated, a large part of Cowper's satire is devoted to the discussion of religious topics. Cowper has the evangelical insistence on the practical and experimental character of religion, and is shocked by worldliness, above all in the clergy:

Occiduus is a pastor of renown;
When he has prayed and preached the sabbath down,
With wire and catgut he concludes the day,
Quavering and semiquavering care away.
The full concerto swells upon your ear;
All elbows shake. Look in, and you would swear
The Babylonian tyrant with a nod
Had summoned them to serve his golden god;
So well that thought the employment seems to suit,
Psaltery and sackbut, dulcimer and flute.
Oh fie! 'Tis evangelical and pure:
Observe each face, how sober and demure!
Ecstasy sets her stamp on every mien;
Chins fallen, and not an eyeball to be seen.
Still I insist, though music heretofore
Has charmed me much, (not even Occiduus more,)
Love, joy, and peace make harmony more meet
For sabbath evenings, and perhaps as sweet.

Will not the sickliest sheep of every flock
Resort to this example as a rock;
There stand and justify the foul abuse
Of sabbath hours, with plausible excuse?
If apostolic gravity be free
To play the fool on Sundays, why not we?
If he the tinkling harpsichord regards
As inoffensive, what offence in cards?
Strike up the fiddles, let us all be gay!
Laymen have leave to dance, if parsons play.

The following portrait of a religious prude is worth comparing with Young's female character sketches:

Yon ancient prude, whose withered features show
She might be young some forty years ago,
Her elbows pinioned close upon her hips,
Her head erect, her fan upon her lips,
Her eyebrows arched, her eyes both gone astray
To watch yon amorous couple in their play,
With bony and unkerchiefed neck defies
The rude inclemency of wintry skies,
And sails with lappet-head and mincing airs,
Duly at clink of bell, to morning prayers.
To thrift and parsimony much inclined,
She yet allows herself that boy behind;
The shivering urchin, bending as he goes,
With slipshod heels, and dew-drop at his nose,
His predecessor's coat advanced to wear,
Which future pages yet are doomed to share,
Carries her Bible tucked beneath his arm,
And hides his hands to keep his fingers warm.
She, half an angel in her own account,
Doubts not hereafter with the saints to mount,
Though not a grace appears on strictest search,
But that she fasts, and, *item*, goes to church.
Conscious of age, she recollects her youth,
And tells, not always with an eye to truth,
Who spanned her waist, and who, where'er he came,
Scrawled upon glass Miss Bridget's lovely name,
Who stole her slipper, filled it with Tokay,
And drank the little bumper every day.
Of temper as envenomed as an asp,
Censorious, and her every word a wasp;

In faithful memory she records the crimes,
Or real or fictitious, of the times;
Laughs at the reputations she has torn,
And holds them dangling at arm's length in scorn.

We have so far said nothing of the tradition of satire in Scottish poetry. It is in fact a strong one, but has different roots from the English tradition we have been dealing with. It rests not so much on the classical Roman satirists, as on the medieval 'flyting'. This was originally an improvised exchange of violent but not necessarily seriously intended abuse. Examples of this kind of thing will be found in the work of **William Dunbar** (1465?–1530?), Skelton's contemporary, and probably the greatest of Scottish poets. Writing in the northern vernacular declined after the accession of James I and VI to the English throne. But it revived in the eighteenth century with the work of **Allan Ramsay** (1686–1758), **Robert Fergusson** (1750–74) and others. The work of **Robert Burns** (1759–96) represents the high point of development of this second Scottish school. Burns's satires are some of his best and most original work. They have a vigour and frankness of language which harks back to the earlier Scottish tradition. *Holy Willie's Prayer* is a blistering attack on religious hypocrisy, and also a portrait of considerable psychological subtlety:

O Thou, wha in the Heavens dost dwell,
Wha, as it pleases best thysel',
Sends ane to heaven and ten to hell,
A' for thy glory,
And no for ony guid or ill
They've done afore thee!

I bless and praise thy matchless might,
When thousands thou hast left in night,
That I am here afore thy sight,
For gifts and grace
A burnin' an' a shinin' light,
To a' this place.

. . . .

But yet O Lord! confess I must
At times I'm fash'd wi' fleshy lust;
An' sometimes too, in warldly trust,
Vile self gets in;
But thou remembers we are dust,
Defiled in sin.

O Lord! yestreen, thou kens, wi' Meg –
Thy pardon I sincerely beg;
O! way't ne'er be a living plague
To my dishonor:
And I'll ne'er lift a lawless leg
Again upon her.

. . . .

Lord, hear my earnest cry an' prayer,
Against that prestbyt'ry of Ayr;
Thy strong right hand, Lord, make it bare
Upo' their heads;
Lord, weigh it down, and dinna spare,
For their misdeeds.

O Lord my God, that glib-tongu'd Aiken,
My very heart and soul are quakin',
To think how we stood sweatin', shakin',
An' pissed wi' dread,
While he, wi' hingin' lips and snakin',
Held up his head.

. . . .

But, Lord, remember me and mine
Wi' mercies temp'ral and divine,
That I for gear and grace may shine
Excelled by nane,
And a' the glory shall be thine,
Amen, Amen!

7

Regency Satire

We now reach the period of the great flowering of Romantic poetry, which begins with the publication of Wordsworth's and Coleridge's *Lyrical Ballads* in 1798, and ends with the death of Byron in 1824. We do not usually associate satire with the Romantic spirit. For satire is essentially a criticism of contemporary society, and assumes a structure of widely shared moral values and beliefs. Romanticism is itself a symptom of the breakdown of such a structure. The Romantic poet is typically isolated and alienated from his society, turned inward on himself, and concerned to construct his own system of values, based largely on private and individual experience. Wordsworth is the greatest of the English Romantic poets; and a satirical or a comic poem from him is unthinkable.

But the Romantics, especially those of the second generation, were also youthful and radical revolutionaries, in an age of rapid change, of revolt and of entrenched reaction. This led them sometimes to speak out with scorn and irony, and Byron, at least, proved to be a major satirical poet. But the best of his satires are of a new type, not deriving from the central Augustan tradition, though owing something to Churchill and to Wolcot.

The Augustan tradition itself, however, died hard. The last major poet (or at least the present writer would accord that status to him) to write within it, and to continue to develop it, was **George Crabbe** (1754–1832). Crabbe has considerable satirical power, but in his more mature and typical work this element is closely integrated with his main design as a narrative poet and realistic observer of nature. Compared with Crabbe, **William Gifford** (1756–1826) is a minor figure, but is of interest as a satirist still working the Augustan vein. His character strikes one as rather disagreeable. Though of humble origins, he was a strong Tory, and in his later years as a reviewer for the *Quarterly* was an enemy of the Romantic poets.[1] His *Baviad* and *Maeviad* deal with a less significant deviation from the Augustan norm. They are an attack on the group of dilettante poetasters known as the Della Cruscans. These were really too

[1] Gifford also became in 1797 the editor of *The Anti-Jacobin*. The satirical verse published in this journal by **George Canning** and others must be mentioned here, but belonged to the field of parody rather than satire proper.

insignificant to merit the savage treatment which Gifford accorded them. The following sketch, from the *Baviad*, of Robert Merry, their leader, is not unamusing. A poetry reading is going on at the house of Mrs. Piozzi (formerly Mrs. Thrale):

> 'Tis done. Her house the generous Piozzi lends,
> And thither summons her blue-stocking friends;
> The summons her blue-stocking friends obey,
> Lured by the love of Poetry and Tea.
> The Bard steps forth, in birth-day splendour drest,
> His right hand graceful waving o'er his breast;
> His left extending, so that all may see,
> A roll inscribed 'The Wreath of Liberty'.
> So forth he steps, and with complacent air,
> Bows round the circle, and assumes the chair;
> With lemonade he gargles next his throat,
> Then sweetly preludes to the liquid note:

The *Maeviad* contains the following malicious portrait of Boswell in his later years:

> And Boswell, aping, with preposterous pride,
> Johnson's worst frailties, rolls from side to side,
> His heavy head from hour to hour erects,
> Affects the fool, and is what he affects.

Byron (1788–1824) is a paradoxical figure. For his own time, and for Europe generally throughout the nineteenth century, he stood as the very embodiment of Romanticism. Yet he himself rejected most of the Romantic poetry of his contemporaries and was a fervent champion of Pope and of Augustan literary values. Moreover it is his satires which have best stood the test of time, and not such romantic narratives as *Childe Harold*, *The Giaour* and *The Corsair*. Byron indeed never regarded these pieces as of very much poetic importance; but they sold, and won him enormous literary fame and popularity. They did in fact express one side of his deeply divided personality. The guilt-ridden, alienated rebel and wanderer which he projects in these poems is not just a pose. But his letters, and the accounts of his conversation, show that Byron also possessed much good humour and good sense, and that there was even a strong tinge of the conventional puritan moralist about him. It was this side of his nature which he strove to express in his satires, which he produced concurrently with his romantic poems throughout his poetical career.

But it was not until he came to write *Don Juan* that he discovered a form wholly adequate to what he had to say. *Don Juan* transcends the limitations of Augustan satire and is something wholly new. It is Byron's greatest work, and he knew that it was. He continued to persevere with it to the end, in spite of the objections of many of his friends, of his mistress, the Countess Guiccoli, and of his publisher, John Murray. They all wanted fresh Harolds, Giaours and Corsairs.

Byron's first published volume was *Hours of Idleness* which appeared in 1807. It was a collection of adolescent verses, conventionally sentimental and romantic. The volume was very severely handled by Jeffrey in *The Edinburgh Review*, partly because Byron had a title, and had made some parade in these poems of his aristocratic and ancient lineage. This rebuff stung Byron into writing the first of his satires, *English Bards and Scotch Reviewers*. In this he showed a quite unexpected command of invective and of the classical heroic couplet. From now on it was clear that here was a poet to be reckoned with; and the continuing pattern of alternating Romanticism and Augustan Classicism which was to run through Byron's work was established.

English Bards is not simply a retort upon Jeffrey and the Whig literary coterie which he represented. It is a survey of the whole contemporary state of the world of letters. Byron declares his allegiance to the ideals of the Augustan age:

Time was, ere yet in these degenerate days
Ignoble themes obtain'd mistaken praise,
When sense and wit with poesy allied,
No fabled graces, flourish'd side by side;
From the same fount their inspiration drew,
And, rear'd by taste, bloom'd fairer as they grew.
Then, in this happy isle, a Pope's pure strain
Sought the rapt soul to charm, nor sought in vain;
A polish'd nation's praise aspired to claim,
And raised the people's, as the poet's fame.
Like him great Dryden pour'd the tide of song,
In stream less smooth, indeed, yet doubly strong.
Then Congreve's scenes could cheer, or Otway's melt –
For nature then an English audience felt.
But why these names, or greater still, retrace,
When all to feebler bards resign their place?
Yet to such times our lingering looks are cast,
When taste and reason with those times are past.

With this Byron contrasts the extravagances of Romanticism, as typified by the early verse romances of Scott:

> Thus Lays of Minstrels – may they be the last! –
> On half-strung harps whine mournful to the blast.
> While mountain spirits prate to river sprites,
> That dames may listen to the sound at nights;
> And goblin brats, of Gilpin Horner's brood,
> Decoy young border-nobles through the wood,
> And skip at every step, Lord knows how high,
> And frighten foolish babes, the Lord knows why;
> While high-born ladies in their magic cell,
> Forbidding knights to read who cannot spell,
> Despatch a courier to a wizard's grave,
> And fight with honest men to shield a knave.

Later on Byron's personal liking for Scott was to make him alter his opinion of his poetry; Tom Moore, who was likewise to become an intimate friend of Byron, also comes in for some scathing criticism in *English Bards*, under his pseudonym of 'Tom Little'. In a later passage of *English Bards* Byron does indeed suggest that Scott is capable of better things:

> And thou, too, Scott! resign to minstrels rude
> The wilder slogan of a border feud:
> Let others spin their meagre lines for hire;
> Enough for genius, if itself inspire!
> Let Southey sing, although his teeming muse,
> Prolific every spring, be too profuse;
> Let simple Wordsworth chime his childish verse,
> And brother Coleridge lull the babe at nurse;
> Let spectre-mongering Lewis aim, at most,
> To rouse the galleries, or raise a ghost;
> Let Moore still sigh; let Strangford steal from Moore,
> And swear that Camoëns sang such notes of yore;
> Let Hayley hobble on, Montgomery rave,
> And godly Grahame chant a stupid stave:
> Let sonneteering Bowles his strains refine,
> And whine and whimper to the fourteenth line;
> Let Stott, Carlisle, Matilda, and the rest
> Of Grub Street, and of Grosvenor Place the best,
> Scrawl on, till death release us from the strain,
> Or Common Sense assert her rights again.
> But thou, with powers that mock the aid of praise,
> Shouldst leave to humbler bards ignoble lays:

Thy country's voice, the voice of all the nine,
Demand a hallow'd harp – that harp is thine.

It will be noticed that in the above passage Byron makes no distinction between the Lake poets and such minor figures as 'Monk' Lewis, Montgomery, 'Laura Matilda' (a Della Cruscan poetess), Hayley (Blake's patron), Bowles and others. Bowles comes in for special castigation elsewhere in the poem, as the critical belittler of Pope. The only contemporary poets whom Byron whole-heartedly praises in *English Bards* are Campbell and Rogers, regarded as continuers of the Augustan tradition. Later on he was to express admiration for Crabbe for the same reason. There are a number of tributes to Gifford, and *The Baviad* and *The Maeviad* are clearly Byron's immediate models. In a passage alluding to the humble birth of both poets Byron makes it clear that he regards Gifford as 'a greater far' than Burns.

Byron was to write several further satires in heroic couplets. These include *Hints from Horace*, *The Waltz*, *The Blues* and *The Age of Bronze*. They deal for the most part with rather transient subjects and lack the personal interest which attaches to *English Bards and Scotch Reviewers*. For all his admiration for Pope, the couplet was really too tight a form to be a suitable vehicle for Byron's satire. It was his discovery of the burlesque possibilities of the *ottava rima* which really furnished him with a form that suited his genius.

The *ottava rima*, a stanza rhyming *abababcc*, had been the metre of the Italian Renaissance epic, employed by Ariosto and Tasso. There is much of the comic spirit in Ariosto, and a delicate irony, but they are never pushed as far as burlesque. This step was taken by his successor **Luigi Pulci** (1432–84) in his *Morgante Maggiore*, a poem closer in spirit to Rabelais than to Ariosto. Byron translated this poem in part. **John Hookham Frere** (1769–1846) imitated the style of Pulci in his *The Monks and the Giants*, and this seems to have been Byron's immediate exemplar. His first exercise in the *ottava rima* was *Beppo*, a comic short story with a Venetian setting, which having completed he launched into *Don Juan.*

Don Juan is, as we have said, something quite new in literature. Yet many traditions, besides the Pulcian burlesque epic, converge in it. Its individual tone and panache owe something to Churchill; its verbal bravura partly derives from Wolcot. Its comic use of double and triple rhymes is in the Hudibrastic tradition. But we must also remember that Byron was an inveterate reader of novels, especially of the great comic novelists of the eighteenth century, and that tradition is also continued in *Don Juan*. *Don Juan* is conceived as a comic epic poem, just as, in prose, are the novels of Fielding. The influence of Smollett and of the picaresque novel in general is also very marked; while from Sterne's *Tristram Shandy* Byron took over the techniques of deliberate digression and rapid shifting of tone.

Don Juan reads like, and to a large extent is, a brilliant improvisation. It has the quality of rapid and informal conversation. The casual tone is established from the start, as when Byron speaks of his fixing on a hero:

I want a hero: an uncommon want,
  When every year and month sends forth a new one,
Till, after cloying the gazettes with cant,
  The age discovers he is not the true one:
Of such as these I should not care to vaunt,
  I'll therefore take our ancient friend Don Juan –
We all have seen him in the pantomime,
Sent to the devil somewhat ere his time.

. . . .

Nelson was once Britannia's god of war,
  And still should be so, but the tide is turn'd;
There's no more to be said of Trafalgar,
  'Tis with our hero quietly inurn'd;
Because the army's grown more popular,
  At which the naval people are concern'd;
Besides, the prince is all for the land-service.
Forgetting Duncan, Nelson, Howe, and Jervis.

Brave men were living before Agamemnon
  And since, exceeding valorous and sage,
A good deal like him too, though quite the same none;
  But then they shone not on the poet's page,
And so have been forgotten: I condemn none,
  But can't find any in the present age
Fit for my poem (that is, for my new one);
So, as I said, I'll take my friend Don Juan.

Most epic poets plunge 'in medias res'
  (Horace makes this the heroic turnpike road),
And then your hero tells, whene'er you please,
  What went before – by way of episode,
While seated after dinner at his ease,
  Beside his mistress in some soft abode,

Palace, or garden, paradise, or cavern,
Which serves the happy couple for a tavern.

That is the usual method, but not mine –
My way is to begin at the beginning;
The regularity of my design
Forbids all wandering as the worst of sinning,
And therefore I shall open with a line
(Although it cost me half an hour in spinning)
Narrating somewhat of Don Juan's father,
And also of his mother, if you'd rather.

Byron knew of Don Juan as a popular hero of pantomime. It is not by any means certain that he knew the play by the sixteenth-century Spanish dramatist Tirso de Molina in which the Don first appears, or Molière's comedy, or Mozart's and Da Ponte's opera on the same subject. The first English treatment of the legend was in Shadwell's play *The Libertine*. This contains an episode in which the hero is shipwrecked and is befriended by a fisher girl, which may just possibly have suggested the Haidee scenes in Byron's poem. Nevertheless Byron's hero is not so much the seducer of the traditional story as the rather passive object of women's desires. Like Voltaire's Candide his adventures in different countries – in Spain, among the Greek islands, in the Sultan's harem, at the court of Catherine the Great, on the battlefield, and finally in fashionable London society – furnish his author with a method of giving a critical view of the whole of contemporary civilization. The unfinished poem breaks off in the middle of an episode, though Byron had declared that his hero was to end in Hell, or married (much the same thing, in Byron's opinion). *Don Juan* does not lend itself easily to brief illustrative quotation. But it contains passages of brilliant and sometimes scathing satire as well as of romantic description and, at least in the Haidee episode, of romantic tenderness. But the all-pervading tone of irony somehow gives to these last passages a concreteness and a lack of sentimentality, which distinguishes them from the popular romantic vein of Byron's other narratives. In *Don Juan*, in fact, the two strains in Byron's writing come together to form a unity.

If *Don Juan* is Byron's greatest work, *The Vision of Judgment* is perhaps the most artistically perfect. It was written while Byron was already engaged upon *Don Juan*, and is in the same stanza. On the occasion of the death of George III in 1820, Southey, as Poet Laureate, had published *A Vision of Judgment*. In this poem, written in hexameters, he celebrated the entry of the deceased monarch's soul into Heaven. The flattery was fulsome, and prompted Byron's ironic satire, the plan of which, as we have already pointed out, was probably suggested by Seneca's *Apocolocyntosis.* St. Peter, watching at the gate of Heaven, is surprised to find the old half-mad king seeking admittance. This is disputed by Satan who debates the king's case with the Archangel Michael. Satan summons a cloud of witnesses against the king, including Wilkes and the shadowy author of *The Letters of Junius.* Finally the wretched Southey is himself brought on the scene, but when he offers to recite his poem in honour of the king, the entire company scatters in consternation:

> He ceased, and drew forth an MS.; and no
> Persuasion on the part of devils, saints,
> Or angels, now could stop the torrent; so
> He read the first three lines of the contents;
> But at the fourth, the whole spiritual show
> Had vanish'd, with variety of scents,
> Ambrosial and sulphureous, as they sprang,
> Like lightning, off from his 'melodious twang'.
>
> Those grand heroics acted as a spell:
> The angels stopp'd their ears and plied their pinions;
> The devils ran howling, deafen'd, down to hell;
> The ghosts fled, gibbering, for their own dominions –
> (For 'tis not yet decided where they dwell,
> And I leave every man to his opinions);
> Michael took refuge in his trump – but, lo!
>
> . . . .
>
> His teeth were set on edge, he could not blow!
> As for the rest, to come to the conclusion
> Of this true dream, the telescope is gone
> Which kept my optics free from all delusion,
> And show'd me that I in my turn have shown;
> All I saw farther, in the last confusion,
> Was, that King George slipp'd into heaven for one;
> And when the tumult dwindled to a calm,
> I left him practising the hundredth psalm.

This poem not only shows Byron's humour at its most lively but also his scorn at its most Olympian, so that his indignation at George III's political misdeeds can even be tempered by a kind of pity and humorous indulgence for the man.

Shelley (1792–1822) is often thought of, in Matthew Arnold's phrase, as a beautiful but ineffectual angel. But there was another side to his nature. He was in fact capable both of humour and of good sense, and his satirical poems are not negligible. *Swellfoot the Tyrant* is a very lively Aristophanic comedy. Its subject is the scandal attending George IV's breach with his wife, and it has a chorus of pigs representing the people of England. The *Letter to Maria Gisborne* is not strictly a satire, but belongs to the tradition of the Horatian epistle. It was written in 1820, while Shelley was staying at the Gisbornes' villa at Leghorn. The metre is the heroic couplet, but treated with the extreme licence of *enjambement* which Shelley and his contemporaries adopted, following the example of some Elizabethan and seventeenth-century poets. At its best this poem captures admirably the tone of colloquial speech. Maria is in London, and Shelley imagines her seeing those literary friends and acquaintances he remembers and reveres:

You are now
In London, that great sea, whose ebb and flow
At once is deaf and loud, and on the shore
Vomits its wrecks, and still howls on for more.
Yet in its depths what treasures! You will see
That which was Godwin, – greater none than he
Though fallen – and fallen on evil times – to stand
Among the spirits of our age and land,
Before the dread tribunal of *to come*
The foremost, – while Rebuke cowers pale and dumb.
You will see Coleridge – he who sits obscure
In the exceeding lustre and the pure
Intense irradiation of a mind,
Which, with its own internal lightning blind,
Flags wearily through darkness and despair –
A cloud-encircled meteor of the air,
A hooded eagle among blinking owls. –

. . . .

and there
Is English Peacock, with his mountain Fair,
Turned into a Flamingo; – that shy bird
That gleams i' the Indian air – have you not heard
When a man marries, dies, or turns Hindoo,
His best friends hear no more of him? – but you
Will see him, and will like him too, I hope,
With the milk-white Snowdonian Antelope

Matched with this cameleopard – his fine wit
Makes such a wound, the knife is lost in it;
A strain too learned for a shallow age,
Too wise for selfish bigots.

Wordsworth's *Peter Bell* appeared in 1819. This highly characteristic, but not wholly successful poem tells the story of an insensitive potter who is eventually converted by the influence of natural objects. It inevitably invited parodies. The first of these was *Peter Bell the Second*, written by Keats's friend John Hamilton Reynolds. This was followed by Shelley's *Peter Bell the Third*. Shelley recognized Wordsworth's greatness, but the poem contains some very cogent criticism of his characteristic faults, as well as of what Shelley and most of the other younger Romantics regarded as his political defection. Shelley's Peter, who is, of course, Wordsworth himself, dies and goes to Hell:

Hell is a city much like London –
  A populous and a smoky city;
There are all sorts of people undone,
And there is little or no fun done;
  Small justice shown, and still less pity.

There is a Castles, and a Canning,
  A Cobbett, and a Castlereagh;
All sorts of caitiff corses planning
All sorts of cozening for trepanning
  Corpses less corrupt than they.

There is a ***, who has lost
His wits, or sold them, none knows which;
He walks about a double ghost,
And though as thin as Fraud almost –
Ever grows more grim and rich.

There is a Chancery Court; a King;
  A manufacturing mob; a set
Of thieves who by themselves are sent
Similar thieves to represent;
  An army; and a public debt.

Peter becomes a literary hanger-on of the Devil. Grace is offered him through his meeting with 'a mighty poet and a subtle-souled psychologist' (Coleridge), who is also a frequenter of the Devil's supper parties. But the Devil manages to circumvent this, and Peter returns to earth to fall into the double demnation of total dullness:

Peter was dull – he was at first
  Dull – oh, so dull – so very dull!
Whether he talked, wrote, or rehearsed –
Still with this dulness was he cursed –
  Dull – beyond all conception – dull.

No one could read his books – no mortal,
  But a few natural friends, would hear him;
The parson came not near his portal;
His state was like that of the immortal
  Described by Swift – no man could bear him.

His sister, wife, and children yawned,
  With a long, slow, and drear ennui,
All human patience far beyond;
Their hopes of Heaven each would have pawned,
  Anywhere else to be.

. . . .

His servant-maids and dogs grew dull;
  His kitten, late a sportive elf;
The woods and lakes, so beautiful,
  Of dim stupidity were full,
  All grew dull as Peter's self.

The finest of Shelley's satirical poems (though it almost transcends that category) is the *Masque of Anarchy*. It was written in a white heat of indignation in 1819, on hearing the news of the so-called Peterloo massacre at Manchester, in which a party of hussars rode down a crowd of peaceful demonstrators. The opening of the poem has an apocalyptic quality, reminiscent of Langland and the medieval tradition. Shelley probably had in mind the pageant of the Seven Deadly Sins in Book I of Spenser's *Faerie Queene*:

I met Murder on the way –
He had a mask like Castlereagh –
Very smooth he looked, yet grim;
Seven blood-hounds followed him:

All were fat; and well they might
Be in admirable plight,
For one by one, and two by two,
He tossed them human hearts to chew
Which from his wide cloak he drew.

Next came Fraud, and he had on,
Like Eldon, an ermined gown;
His big tears, for he wept well,
Turned to mill-stones as they fell.

And the little children, who
Round his feet played to and fro,
Thinking every tear a gem,
Had their brains knocked out by them.

Clothed with the Bible, as with light,
And the shadows of the night,
Like Sidmouth, next, Hypocrisy
On a crocodile rode by.

And many more Destructions played
In this ghastly masquerade,
All disguised, even to the eyes,
Like Bishops, lawyers, peers, or spies.

Last came Anarchy: he rode
On a white horse, splashed with blood;
He was pale even to the lips,
Like Death in the Apocalypse.

And he wore a kingly crown;
And in his grasp a sceptre shone;
On his brow this mark I saw –
'I am God, and King, and Law!'

Keats (1795–1821) left *The Cap and Bells*, his attempt at a mock-heroic poem, unfinished at his death. It has, I think, been rather neglected and undervalued. It comes as a bit of a shock to Keats's more earnest admirers to find that after the achievement of the Odes, and the tremendous promise of *Hyperion*, his last work should be a rather frivolous one. Keats was probably prompted by the example of Byron's *Don Juan*. But his choice of the Spenserian stanza, instead of the *ottava rima*, was not a fortunate one. The Spenserian stanza is by nature diffuse and slow moving, and hence not well adapted to satire. Nevertheless, the poem has passages of humour, fancy, and at times, real poetry. Its subject, like that of Shelley's *Swellfoot*, is the scandals attending George IV's breach with Queen Caroline. The King appears as the fairy emperor Elfinan. Disturbed by his penchant for mortal maidens, his Parliament insists on his marrying the Princess Bellanaine, daughter of the King of the Pygmies.

D

Elfinan, however, remains in pursuit of Bertha (who had been the romantic heroine of Keat's unfinished *Eve of St. Mark*). As an example of Keats's satire we may quote the stanzas describing Elfinan's rage at his Parliament:

'I'll trounce some of the members', cried the Prince,
I'll put a mark against some rebel names,
I'll make the Opposition-benches wince,
I'll show them very soon, to all their shames,
What 'tis to smother up a Prince's flames;
That ministers should join in it, I own,
Surprises me! – they too at these high games!
Am I an Emperor? Do I wear a crown?
Imperial Elfinan, go hang thyself or drown!

'I'll trounce 'em! – there's the square-cut chancellor,
His son shall never touch that bishopric;
And for the nephew of old Palfior,
I'll show him that his speeches made me sick,
And give the colonelcy to Phalaric;
The tiptoe Marquis, moral and gallant,
Shall lodge in shabby taverns upon tick;
And for the Speaker's second cousin's aunt,
She sha'n't be maid of honour, – by heaven that she sha'n't!

'I'll shirk the Duke of A.; I'll cut his brother;
I'll give no garter to his eldest son;
I won't speak to his sister or his mother!
The Viscount B. shall live at cut-and-run;
But how in the world can I contrive to stun
That fellow's voice, which plagues me worse than any,
That stubborn fool, that impudent state-dun,
Who sets down ev'ry sovereign as a zany, –
That vulgar commoner, Esquire Biancopany?

Praed (1802–39) is more of a writer of elegant and witty light verse than a satirist. He became a member of Sir Robert Peel's administration, and in *The New Order of Things* he pokes gentle fun at the Whigs' pretensions to be reformers:

We used to fancy Englishmen
Had broken Europe's chain,
And won a battle now and then
Against the French in Spain;
Oh no! we never ruled the waves,
Whatever people say;

We've all been despicable slaves:
The Whigs are in to-day!

It's time for us to see the things
Which other folk have seen;
It's time we should cashier our kings,
And build our guillotine;
We'll abrogate Police and Peers,
And vote the Church away;
We'll hang the parish overseers:
The Whigs are in to-day!

We'll put the landlords to the rout,
We'll burn the College Halls,
We'll turn St. James's inside out
And batter down St. Paul's.
We'll hear no more of Bench or Bar;
The troops shall have no pay;
We'll turn adrift our men-of-war:
The Whigs are in to-day!

Praed is perhaps at his best when dealing with the foibles of fashionable society, as in *Goodnight to the Season*:

Good night to the Season! – the dances,
The fillings of hot little rooms,
The glancing of rapturous glances,
The fancying of fancy costumes;
The pleasures which fashion makes duties,
The praisings of fiddles and flutes,
The luxury of looking at Beauties,
The tedium of talking to mutes;
The female diplomatists, planners
Of matches for Laura and Jane;
The ice of her Ladyship's manners,
The ice of his Lordship's champagne.

Good night to the Season! – the rages
Led off by the chiefs of the throng,
The Lady Matilda's new pages,
The Lady Eliza's new song;
Miss Fennel's macaw, which at Boodle's
Was held to have something to say;
Miss Splenetic's musical poodles,
Which bark '*Batti Batti*' all day;

The pony Sir Araby sported,
  As hot and black as a coal,
And the Lion his mother imported,
  In bearskins and grease, from the Pole.

There is an undercurrent of nostalgic feeling as well as of wit here. The elegance and lightness of touch of which Praed is an exponent were something which was to evaporate from English poetry as the Victorian age came on.

8

The Victorians

The Victorians did not give a high place to poetic satire. In general they excluded the elements of wit and humour from serious poetry. The achievement of the Augustan poets was undervalued, so that eventually Matthew Arnold could declare that Dryden and Pope were not classics of our poetry but classics of our prose. Humour and satire tended to be relegated to a special and inferior category of light verse, with no poetic pretensions. The Victorian light verse tradition is represented by such figures as **Hood** (1799–1845), **Barham** (1788–1845), **Thackeray** (1811–63), and **W. S. Gilbert** (1836–1911). These do not really concern us here, though Hood was at least, at times, a true poet, in the Romantic tradition. His longest poem, *Miss Kilmansegg and her Precious Leg*, whose theme is the vulgarity of the new commercial monied class, comes near to being true satire.

Tennyson (1809–92), though he generally wore the poet's mantle with self-conscious solemnity, was not without a sense of humour. But it took an affront to his self-esteem to goad him into a piece of really powerful satiric invective. This happened when **Bulwer-Lytton** (1803–73) published a satirical poem entitled *The New Timon*. In it he characterized the poets of the time and included the following lines:

'Not mine, not mine (O muse forbid) the boon
Of borrow'd notes, the mock-bird's modish tune,
The jingling medley of purloined conceits,
Out-babying Wordsworth and out-glittering Keats;
Where all the airs of patchwork pastoral chime
To drown the ears in Tennysonian rhyme!

'Let school-miss Alfred vent her chaste delight
On "darling little rooms so warm and light;"
Chant "I'm a-weary" in infectious strain,
And catch "the blue fly singing i' the pane;"
Though praised by critics and adored by Blues,
Though Peel with pudding plump the puling muse,
Though Theban taste the Saxon purse controls,
And pensions Tennyson while starves a Knowles.'

Lytton refers to two poems in Tennyson's volume of 1830, the mawkish *The Darling Room*, and *Mariana* (actually one of Tennyson's finest) with its recurrent refrain 'she said "I am aweary . . ."'. The last line may be thought by the modern reader distinctly to have misfired. Sheridan Knowles is a now almost totally forgotten dramatic poet.

Always hyper-sensitive to criticism, Tennyson retorted with *The New Timon and the Poets*. This appeared in *Punch*, 28 February 1846, over the signature 'Alcibiades'. The poem has a fine scorn:

'We know him, out of *Shakespeare's* art,
  And those fine curses which he spoke;
The old Timon, with his noble heart,
  That, strongly loathing, greatly broke.

'So died the Old; here comes the New.
  Regard him: a familiar face:
I *thought* we knew him: What, it's you,
  The padded man – that wears the stays –

'Who kill'd the girls, and thrill'd the boys,
  With dandy pathos when you wrote,
A Lion, you, that made a noise,
  And shook a mane *en papilotes*.

'And once you tried the Muses too;
  You fail'd, Sir; therefore now you turn,
You fall on those who are to you
  As Captain is to Subaltern.

'But men of long-enduring hopes,
  And careless what this hour may bring,
Can pardon little would-be POPES
  And BRUMMELS, when they try to sting.

. . . .

'What profits now to understand
  The merits of a spotless shirt –
A dapper boot – a little hand –
  If half the little soul is dirt?

'*You* talk of tinsel! – why we see
  The old mark of rouge upon your cheeks.
You prate of Nature! you are he
  That split his life about the cliques.

'A *TIMON* you! Nay, nay for shame:
It looks too arrogant a jest –
The fierce old man – to take *his* name.'
You bandbox. Off, and let him rest.'

Tennyson's *The Princess*, 1847, in which he discusses the question of higher education for women, under the guise of a romantic phantasy, must be mentioned here in passing. It really belongs to the tradition of the mock-heroic poem, but in it the element of satire is largely replaced by that of sentiment.

In the work of **Browning** (1812–89) there is often a considerable element of humour, frequently fantastic, sometimes grim. Mr. J. M. Cohen has pointed out Browning's debt to the grotesque tradition of Hood and Barham. Satire enters into such a dramatic monologue as *Soliloquy of The Spanish Cloister* and also into those which are basically studies of contemporary personalities whom Browning disliked. These last include *Bishop Blougram's Apology, Mr. Sludge the Medium* and *Prince Hohenstiel-Schwangau.* They are based respectively on the characters of Cardinal Wiseman, the American spiritualist Daniel D. Home, and Napoleon III. *A Lost Leader* is in part an attack on Wordsworth for his political change of front, but it should be noted that this is also a dramatic monologue. Wordsworth's shift from radicalism to conservatism had in fact occurred more than a generation before the poem was written, and Browning is putting himself imaginatively in the place of one of Wordsworth's younger contemporaries. Browning did, however, produce one notable piece of direct invective. As in the case of Tennyson's *The New Timon*, it owed its origin to the poet's being touched on a sensitive spot. Edward FitzGerald's posthumous letters contained a sentence to the effect that he 'thanked God that Mrs. Browning was dead'. FitzGerald was probably only expressing his impatience at Mrs. Browning's poetry (an impatience with which some readers may be tempted to sympathize). It was tactless of his executors to allow the sentence to stand while Browning was alive. He was naturally hurt, and expressed his anger in a poem which is still half comic:

I chanced upon a new book yesterday:
I opened it, and, where my finger lay
'Twixt page and uncut page, these words I read
– Some six or seven at most – and learned thereby
That you, Fitzgerald, whom by ear and eye
She never knew, 'thanked God my wife was dead.'

Ay, dead! and were yourself alive, good Fitz,
How to return you thanks would task my wits:
    Kicking you seems the common lot of curs –
    While more appropriate greeting lends you grace:
Surely to spit there glorifies your face –
    Spitting from lips once sanctified by Hers.

The themes of the Odes of **Coventry Patmore** (1823–96) are for the most part human and divine love. But when he comments on contemporary events his scorn, prompted by an extreme high Toryism, has something of the quality of Juvenalian satire. The subject of *1867* is the Reform Bill of that year. Subsequently in his note to this poem Patmore said:

In this year the middle and upper classes were disenfranchised by Mr. Disraeli's Government, and the final destruction of the liberties of England by the Act of 1884 rendered inevitable.

Readers today will hardly sympathize with Patmore's standpoint, and the gibe at Disraeli's Jewish origins is offensive and unworthy; but the poem cannot be denied its prophetic power:

  In the year of the great crime,
When the false English Nobles and their Jew,
By God demented, slew
The Trust they stood twice pledged to keep from wrong,
One said, Take up thy Song,
That breathes the mild and almost mythic time
Of England's prime!
But I, Ah, me,
The freedom of the few
That, in our free Land, were indeed the free,
Can song renew?
Ill singing 'tis with blotting prison-bars,
How high soe'er, betwixt us and the stars;
Ill singing 'tis when there are none to hear;
And days are near
When England shall forget
The fading glow which, for a little while,
Illumes her yet,
The lovely smile
That grows so faint and wan,
Her people shouting in her dying ear,
Are not two daws worth two of any swan!

. . . .

And, now, because the dark comes on apace,
When none can work for fear,
And Liberty in every Land lies slain,
And the two Tyrannies unchallenged reign,
And heavy prophecies, suspended long
At supplication of the righteous few,
And so discredited, to fulfilment throng,
Restrain'd no more by faithful prayer or tear,
And the dread baptism of blood seems near
That brings to the humbled Earth the Time of Grace,
Breathless be song,
And let Christ's own look through
The darkness, suddenly increased,
To the gray secret lingering in the East.

The two hexameter poems of **Clough** (1819–61), *The Bothie* and *Amours de Voyage*, are partly in the mock-heroic tradition and partly short realistic novels in verse. Clough was inspired to write *The Bothie* after reading Longfellow's *Evangeline* aloud to his sister. He saw that the English hexameter had comic potentialities, though that was not what Longfellow had intended. The poem deals with the adventures of a group of Oxford undergraduates on a reading party in the Scottish Highlands, and incidentally discusses many of the social questions of the day. *Amours de Voyage* is in the form of a series of letters supposed to be written by some English tourists who are caught in Italy at the time of Garibaldi's siege of Rome. The following passage will illustrate Clough's colloquial and ironic style:

Now supposing the French or the Neapolitan soldier
Should by some evil chance come exploring the Maison Serny,
(Where the family English are all to assemble for safety,)
Am I prepared to lay down my life for the British female?
Really, who knows? One has bowed and talked, till, little by little,
All the natural heat has escaped of the chivalrous spirit.
Oh, one conformed, of course; but one doesn't die for good manners,
Stab or shoot, or be shot, by way of a graceful attention.
No, if it should be at all, it should be on the barricades there;
Should I incarnadine ever this inky pacifical finger,
Sooner far should it be for this vapour of Italy's freedom,
Sooner far by the side of the d——d and dirty plebeians.
Ah, for a child in the street I could strike; for the full-blown lady –
Somehow, Eustace, alas! I have not felt the vocation.

Clough's best-known satirical poem is *The Latest Decalogue* which gives a withering statement of the real morality of a commercial society:

Thou shalt have one God only; who
Would be at the expense of two?
No graven images may be
Worshipped, except the currency:
Swear not at all; for, for thy curse
Thine enemy is none the worse:
At church on Sunday to attend
Will serve to keep the world thy friend:
Honour thy parents; that is, all
From whom advancement may befall:
Thou shalt not kill; but needst not strive
Officiously to keep alive:
Do not adultery commit;
Advantage rarely comes of it:
Thou shalt not steal; an empty feat,
When it's so lucrative to cheat:
Bear not false witness; let the lie
Have time on its own wings to fly:
Thou shalt not covet; but tradition
Approves all forms of competition.
The sum of all is, thou shalt love,
If any body, God above:
At any rate shall never labour
More than thyself to love thy neighbour.

Alfred Austin (1835–1913) succeeded Tennyson as Poet Laureate and has generally been accounted one of the more disastrous appointees to that curious office. The official poems which he wrote as Laureate merit this judgement, but his early satirical verse in the style of Pope has, in fact, real virtues. As a critic he was a champion of Augustan poetic values at a time when they were generally depreciated. *The Season* sets out to survey the world of fashionable London society. The following passage on the opera is of interest as showing the impact of Verdi's *La Traviata* on Victorian audiences:

The curtain lifts. Behold the 'Lost One' lain
'Mid all the woes of suitors and champagne:
Of the whole crowd the cynosure and queen,
The best-dressed woman in this sumptuous scene.
Wit – beauty – bearing – graciousness – restraint,
Gifts few possess and none can wholly feint;

Not wife, yet woman – hurt, but not debased –
If vain, unselfish – modest, if not chaste;
Wealth, worship, fashion, prostrate at her feet,
Yet fled with Alfred to profound retreat –
For him the World abandoned quite, again
For him endured the pantomime of men –
Her life's one chance, one yearning, straight foregone,
To save the father, sister, in the son –
Wronged, as can wrong alone a lover's skill,
For her fidelity, yet faithful still –
Doomed by disease which modifies, not mars,
Dying like light in some transparent vase –
At last in Alfred's penitent embrace,
Held to his heart and fondled to his face –
Clinging to life, but with untroubled tone
Claiming the Heaven of Virgins for her own –
Is not this, nothing heightened, nothing glozed,
The vocal Drama but this instant closed?
Hark! how fresh plaudits plaudits fresh repeat,
And purest posies kiss the 'Lost One's' feet!

Austin discounts this sentimentalization of the prostitute's life and in the passage which follows shows himself a practical and advanced social moralist:

What is the spell that 'twixt a saint and sinner
The difference makes? a sermon? bah! a dinner.
The odds and ends our silken Claras waste
Would keep our calico Clarissas chaste.
Celia! the lace from off your parasol
Had held Celinda's sunburnt virtue whole:
A hundred pounds would coy have made the nude,
A thousand pounds the prostitute a prude,
A little more expenditure of pelf
Fanny a bigot bitter as yourself!

Hence! surpliced sophists! who with fasts and cries
Would fain compel Omniscience to be wise!
What if, instead of craving drought or rain,
You built a reservoir or delved a drain?
Instead of prayers and platitudes demure,
Diffused the wealth that keeps peers' daughters pure?

. . . .

This earth is man's: not God's, *except* as man's:
And man's the action in it that He plans.
True to his scheme, He never intervenes:
The end being human, human are the means.
What is man's end? To know and to be free.
Think you to compass it by tracts and tea?
Labour is prayer – the only prayer that serves –
And all beside it but disordered nerves.

Austin sees balls as merely a cover for putting girls on the marriage market. To illustrate the harm done by marriages arranged merely for motives of social and financial advancement he tells the story of Blanche Darley. The description of Blanche in her youthful innocence is charming, and shows Austin to be more than a mere *pasticheur*:

You knew Blanche Darley? could we but once more
Behold that belle and pet of '54!
Not e'en a whisper, vagrant up to Town
From hunt or race-ball, augured her renown.
Far in the wolds sequestered life she led,
Fair and unfettered as the fawn she fed:
Caressed the calves, coquetted with the colts,
Bestowed much tenderness on turkey poults,
Bullied the huge ungainly bloodhound pup,
Tiffed with the terrier, coaxed to make it up:
The farmers quizzed about the ruined crops,
The fall of barley, and the rise of hops:
Gave their wives counsel, but gave flannel too,
Present where'er was timely deed to do;
Known, loved, applauded, prayed for far and wide –
The wandering sunshine of the countryside.
So soft her tread, no nautilus that skims
With sail more silent than her liquid limbs.
Her hair so golden that, did slanting eve
With a stray curl its sunlight interweave,
Smit with surprise, you gazed but could not guess
Which the warm sunbeam, which the warmer tress.
Her presence was low music: when she went,
She left behind a dreamy discontent,
As sad as silence when a song is spent.

But Blanche is married to the old and dissolute Lord Vaux:

Vaux has proposed. Vaux! reeking from the stews;
That remnant, Vaux! shrunk, tottering, palsied, wan!

An Earl by right, by courtesy a man.
That soldier-sycophant, with seam and scar
Gashed deep, but not in battle's joyful jar!
He with the cannon's never blent his breath,
Nor gaily galloped up the gaps of death;
Too rich to roam, in bloodless fields and fights
A lie at Brooks's, black-ball drops at White's.
Senilely supple if you lure or warn,
Now prowls the Quadrant, now confers with Kahn.

Romantic boys! be still. Will angry names
Like 'battered beast' annul an Earldom's claims?
Life is not wholly sentiment and stars:
Venus wed Mercury as well as Mars.

Her marriage is, naturally, unhappy. Too late she finds a man she can really love and this leads to scandal and divorce.

We have quoted from Austin rather extensively, but perhaps this may serve a little to redress the balance in regard to his reputation. At least his satire shows that the classical couplet still had possibilities.

9

The Moderns

The poets of the modern period have not made that sharp distinction between satire and serious poetry which characterized the Victorian attitude. On the contrary, wit and humour are now themselves seen as potentially serious elements in poetry, as they had been in the seventeenth century. Satire and irony are found almost everywhere in the best poetry of the twentieth century, though organically fused with other constituents. A complete survey of the satiric element in contemporary poetry would extend the bounds of this chapter unduly. We shall content ourselves by quoting some examples which seem to be of special interest, and which demonstrate a relationship to earlier satiric traditions.

The shift from nineteenth century modes of expression to the manner characteristic of modern poetry did not really take place till about the time of the First World War. Such writers of an older generation as **Rudyard Kipling** (1865–1936) and **Hilaire Belloc** (1870–1953) could write effective satires, but their work in this vein does not rise above the rhetoric of verse to the imaginative seriousness of poetry. It was, perhaps, the experience of war which first showed poets that bitter irony could be used by way of protest in a situation fundamentally tragic. Some of the war poems of **Siegfried Sassoon** (1886–1966) illustrate this; Sassoon also wrote satires during the post-war period, but they are rather lightweight.

However, the most pervasive literary influence on the tone of the new poetry was that of **T. S. Eliot** (1888–1965). Eliot's use of irony derives partly from the seventeenth-century English poets, and partly from the French poet Jules Laforgue (1860–87). Eliot admired Dryden and Pope, but does not seem to have thought that they provided suitable models for a modern poet. In his introduction to the *Selected Poems* of Ezra Pound Eliot tells the following story:

> I remember that Pound once induced me to destroy what I thought an excellent set of couplets; for, said he, 'Pope has done this so well that you cannot do it better; and if you mean this as a burlesque, you had better suppress it, for you cannot parody Pope unless you can write better verse than Pope – and you can't'.

Some later poets who have attempted to use the couplet in the Augustan manner might well have profited from this advice.

As an example of Eliot's satire we may take *The Hippopotamus*. Prefixed to this poem is a quotation from St. Paul's Epistles:

And when this epistle is read among you, cause that it be read also in the church of the Laodiceans.

Laodicea is the church condemned in the Book of Revelation as being neither hot nor cold. The poem, therefore, seems ironically to suggest that the inarticulate mass of humanity, symbolized by the hippopotamus, may be more capable of salvation than the comfortably and conventionally religious. This is reinforced by a metre suggestive of Protestant hymnody:

I saw the 'potamus take wing
Ascending from the damp savannas,
And quiring angels round him sing
The praise of God, in loud hosannas.

. . .

He shall be washed as white as snow,
By all the martyr'd virgins kist,
While the True Church remains below
Wrapt in the old miasmal mist.

The two satirical poems of **James Joyce** (1882–1941), *On the Burner* and *The Holy Office*, are indignant personal retorts to those who accused him of obscenity and tried to have his works suppressed. We quote part of *The Holy Office*, in which Joyce defines his function in relation to the literature of his time. The manner and imagery are somewhat Swiftian – for Swift loomed large in Joyce's Dublin pantheon:

Myself unto myself will give
This name, Katharsis-Purgative.
I, who dishevelled ways forsook
To hold the poets' grammar-book,
Bringing to tavern and to brothel
The mind of witty Aristotle,
Lest bards in the attempt should err
Must here be my interpreter:
Wherefore receive now from my lip
Peripatetic scholarship.
To enter heaven, travel hell,
Be piteous or terrible
One positively needs the ease
Of plenary indulgences.

For every true-born mysticist
A Dante is, unprejudiced,
Who safe at ingle-nook, by proxy,
Hazards extremes of heterodoxy,
Like him who finds a joy at table
Pondering the uncomfortable.
Ruling one's life by common sense
How can one fail to be intense?

. . . .

So distantly I turn to view
The shamblings of that motley crew,
Those souls that hate the strength that mine has
Steeled in the school of old Aquinas.
Where they have crouched and crawled and prayed
I stand, the self-doomed, unafraid,
Unfellowed, friendless and alone,
Indifferent as the herring-bone,
Firm as the mountain-ridges where
I flash my antlers on the air.
Let them continue as is meet
To adequate the balance-sheet.
Though they may labour to the grave
My spirit shall they never have
Nor make my soul with theirs as one
Till the Mahamanvantara be done:
And though they spurn me from their door
My soul shall spurn them evermore.

The term Mahamanvantara in Hindu thought is the Great Year, the cycle of human history which ends and begins anew when Vishnu wakes from his eternal dream. This concept is a governing factor in the structure of *Finnegan's Wake*.

Wyndham Lewis (1884–1957) gave an important place to satire in his theory of literature. His most ambitious exercise in that vein is *The Apes of God*, which is in prose. *One-Way Song* is a poem, in which Lewis expounds one of his characteristic themes – the idea that modern Western civilization is time-bound. The One-ways are those who are imprisoned by this time obsession, one of the symptoms of which is the popular belief in progress:

'Habe die Ehre!' How we One-ways stink
Of progress! I could tell you by your smell!
The effluvium of progress suits you well

Allow me to say sir! (to the perfume born
Of an 'expanding universe', a bursting corn –
An ever-budding, bigger and better, system –
Where no one's ever missed a cosmic bus – or missed 'em
Only because strap-hangers blocked the portals
To get more air, the antisocial mortals –
Yet bigger and better buses every minute
Roar forth. Before you know it you are in it!
One hefty public carriage packed to the brim
With One-ways, Kruschensalted to get slim).
Stagnation has its must. But it's most odd
That *stuffy* odour all One-ways have got!
One would hardly have thought that progress such as ours
Would have made us smell like bloody hot-house flowers!

This poem is in the heroic couplet, but the versification is excessively harsh. One is forced to the conclusion that Lewis did not very well understand the medium in which he was working.

The South African-born poet **Roy Campbell** (1902–57) was a friend and disciple of Wyndham Lewis. He published a good deal of satirical verse throughout his career. Some of it, notably the later pieces, is marked by violence and personal animosity. His targets are mostly left-wing writers and intellectuals. His two earlier satires, *The Wayzgoose* and *The Georgiad*, still retain a good deal of vitality, though the literary quarrels from which they took their rise are now largely a matter of history. Both poems are written in the heroic couplet, in the manner of Dryden, which inevitably gives to them a certain air of *pastiche*. Each of them has a narrative thread, and hence they may be considered as belonging to the mock-heroic tradition; this narrative thread is however in each case comparatively slight. *The Wayzgoose* is an attack on the literary and artistic coteries of South Africa. The scene is supposed to be a literary gathering for a picnic on the veldt:

Two Art Academies arrived in troops
And Durban sent its literary 'groups' –
All who upon the wings of 'uplift' rise
To boost colonial culture to the skies,
All whom their own sarcastic fates pursue
To write for 'Voorslag' or the 'S.A.Q.' –
Statesmen-philosophers with earnest souls,
Whose lofty theories embrace the Poles,
Yet only prove their minds are full of Holes,
And public orators, each one of whom

Had talked both Boer and Briton to their doom,
And slain, the feat of Samson to surpass,
Whole thousands with the jawbone of an ass –
The pale blue Naiads from their streams of ink
With pale blue stockings, such as never shrink,
With pale blue spectacles and pale blue stays,
And pale blue insight into human ways –
Nymphs of the novel, pert and picturesque,
And wooden hamadryads of the desk –
All these came flocking to the scene, and more
Whom to describe would only be a bore.

The reference to statesmen-philosophers is particularly to General Smuts, who gave the name of 'holism' to his philosophical system. Campbell's attack on South African racialism makes a point which it is still relevant to quote today:

Is it the sign of a 'superior race'
To whine to have 'the nigger kept in place'?
Where is his place save in his strength and sense,
And will he stand aside for impotence,
Does Evolution wait for those who lag
Or curtsy to a cheap colonial flag?
Is this 'White Labour' – lolling on this stool,
Fed by a black with every needful tool,
The white man sits and uses but his hands,
The black man does the thinking while he stands:
Five years in long apprenticeship were passed
Ere, fit to loaf, the white emerged at last,
And yet in kicks and blows the black must pay
Unless he learns the business in a day.

The Georgiad, written after Campbell had left South Africa for England, deals in much the same manner with London literary cliques. The title of the poem derives from the so-called Georgian school of poets. Strictly speaking this term applies to the poets who appeared in the Georgian anthologies edited by Edward Marsh between 1910 and 1924. But the term neo-Georgian was used to describe a rather later generation, whose sponsors were Sir John Squire and Edward Shanks. These, along with the inhabitants of literary Bloomsbury, and the frequenters of weekend conferences, are Campbell's targets. The affectation of the Georgians and their successors for rural England, and their cult of the pub, are thus scathingly summed up:

Now hawthorn blooms above the daisied slope
Where lovelorn poets after milkmaids grope,
Or troop whore-hunting down the country lanes
With flashing spectacles and empty brains,
To hang their trousers on the flowering spray
And sport with lousy gypsies in the hay.

. . . .

Others in London sigh with equal force
For Sussex downs and whiffs of Kentish gorse,
And though the trains puff out from morn till eve,
Vastly prefer to stay at home and grieve.
Some to the pubs, muffled like bolshies, go
To sink themselves into a fit of woe:
These are the guys that find the world forlorn
And wish (correctly) they had not been born:
Blaspheming all the universal plan
Because their tart prefers some better man,
Each loves to sit there and astronomise
The floating specks that swim before his eyes,
His world a dream, his life a trickle of stout,
With sleeps between, and death for chucker-out.

Campbell throughout the poem accuses his victims of sexual irregularities and deviations, and in the following passage ridicules the current fashion for the New Psychology:

These navigators, lubberly and sick,
Sail all by theory – they know the trick –
For truth in obvious things is never found
But only hid in the obscure profound:
The well-known capes that on the skyline swerve,
The stars that guide us, and the winds that serve –
At these old fads they never deign to look,
And as for reefs, they are not in the book,
But down below, invisible and dim,
The complexes in soft inertia swim,
Huge useless squids that out of shame or fright
Have sunk insulted from the conscious light –
To these their zigzag courses are related,
By these each ship of fools is navigated.

The political concerns of the nineteen-thirties produced many essays in verse satire, not all of which survive the initial topicality of their subject-matter. There is a strong satirical element in many of the poems written by **W. H. Auden** (b. 1907), **Louis MacNeice** (1907–63), **Edgell Rickword** (b. 1898), **William Plomer** (b. 1903), and others in this period. Auden's *Letter to Lord Byron* first appeared in *Letters from Iceland*, a book produced jointly with MacNeice. Auden uses the Byronic manner to discuss at random the topics of the day. He begins by apostrophizing the master thus:

Excuse, my lord, the liberty I take
   In thus addressing you. I know that you
Will pay the price of authorship and make
   The allowances an author has to do.
   A poet's fan-mail will be nothing new.
And then a lord – Good Lord, you must be peppered,
Like Gary Cooper, Couglin, or Dick Sheppard,

With notes from perfect strangers starting, 'Sir,
   I liked your lyrics, but *Childe Harold's* trash,'
'My daughter writes, should I encourage her?'
   Sometimes containing frank demands for cash,
   Sometimes sly hints at a platonic pash,
And sometimes, though I think this rather crude,
The correspondent's photo in the rude.

And as for manuscripts – by every post. . . .
   I can't improve on Pope's shrill indignation,
But hope that it will please his spiteful ghost
   To learn the use in culture's propagation
   Of modern methods of communication;
New roads, new rails, new contacts, as we know
From documentaries by the G.P.O.

For since the British Isles went Protestant
   A church confession is too high for most.
But still confession is a human want,
   So Englishmen must make theirs now by post
   And authors hear them over breakfast toast.
For, failing them, there's nothing but the wall
Of public lavatories on which to scrawl.

So if ostensibly I write to you
   To chat about your poetry or mine,
There're many other reasons: though it's true
   That I have, at the age of twenty-nine
   Just read *Don Juan* and I found it fine.
I read it on the boat to Reykjavik
Except when eating or asleep or sick.

The stanza form used here is not, however, the *ottava rima*. Auden has adapted the seven line Troilus stanza or rime-royal. In so doing he is able to avoid a sense of the rhyme being forced which sometimes mars Byron's style.

Another poet of the thirties was **Julian Bell** (1908–37), who met his death while serving as an ambulance driver for the Republican side in the Spanish Civil War. In his *New Writing in Europe* Mr. John Lehmann says that 'Pope gradually came to be Bell's greatest admiration in English poetry'. Of his poem *Arms and the Man* Mr. Lehmann goes on to say that it is 'a long and clever essay in the Popean manner, attacking the automatic mechanisms and thought processes in modern society which he believed led to war, and appealing against them to reason'. Bell's *An Epistle on the Subject of the Ethical and Aesthetic Beliefs of Herr Ludwig Wittgenstein* is a satire on the philosopher whose teaching was becoming influential in the Cambridge of Bell's undergraduate days. Wittgenstein who was of Viennese birth and died in 1951, is an important figure in the history of contemporary philosophy, and influenced the rise of logical positivism. He held that the only meaningful statements are those which are empirically verifiable, and that judgements of value, whether ethical or aesthetic, merely signify an emotional preference. Bell says in a note:

> This satire is not intended as a personal attack, nor as a criticism of the purely logical and philosophical achievements of Dr. Wittgenstein, but solely as a criticism of certain views on art and morals advocated by him.

Actually, he goes rather futher than this, and criticizes, with considerable acuteness, Wittgenstein's general position, from the standpoint of a more traditional type of rationalism:

> With privileged omniscience soaring high
> He reads as easy as a watches hand.
> Each whirling, lost electrons motion planned
> He reads as easy as a watch's hand.
> Seeing at once each individual fact,
> Knowing the consequence of every act,
> Plotting a graph on spaces winding curves,
> Conscious that instant if one atom swerves.
> Knows too the black depths of the human mind,
> Motive and thought their name, shape, cause assigned;
> The highest ecstasy, most black despair,
> Moments when beauty lights the laden air;
> Moments when lovers part, or when they meet, –

Omniscient Wittgenstein grows indiscreet:
Knows every stray reflection, joke and whim,
Hopes, fears and fancies, all are known to him.
Yet, though he searches every thought and shape
The flying values from the net escape.

Later on he accuses Wittgenstein of reintroducing religious and mystical concepts, smuggling them in, as it were, by the back door.

Bell's use of the heroic couplet in this poem is not uniformly successful. Sometimes it comes too near mere *pastiche* of Pope's manner, and at others presents awkward turns of phrase which Pope would never have tolerated.

Hugh MacDiarmid (b. 1892), our most distinguished living Scottish poet, has, in some of his poems, revived the distinctively Scottish satiric note. His *Your Immortal Memory, Burns* is not really an attack on Burns's reputation (though MacDiarmid does, I think, believe it to have been inflated, by comparison with the great Scottish poets of the fifteenth century). The poem is a satire on the bourgeois cult of 'Rabbie Burns', as an excuse for Burns-Night dinners:

Though may demit
Its functions fit
While still to thee, O Burns,
The punctual stomach of thy people turns.

Most folks agree
That poetry
Is of no earthly use
Save thine – which yields at least this Annual Excuse!

Other cults die:
But who'll deny
That you your mob in thrall
Will keep, O Poet Intestinal?

. . . .

Belly will praise
Thee all its days
And spread to all nations
Thy fame in belchings and regurgitations,

While mean minds soar
And hiccoughs adore
And butcher-meat faces
Triumphant, transfigured, example thy graces!

'Daughter of holy Themis and goat-footed Pan' – so a German poet has apostrophized satire. The phrase, if a little portentous, does express very well that union of the moral sense with the comic spirit which characterizes satire at its best. The line of satiric poetry in English literature has been strong and continuous. It has been closely linked to our traditions of political and individual freedom. The present survey has necessarily brought in a good deal of English political and social history. It is hoped that it has also provided entertainment as well as instruction.

Critical Books for Further Reading

J. W. DUFF *Roman Satire, its Outlook on Social Life.* University of California Press, 1936.

GILBERT HIGHET *The Classical Tradition.* Clarendon Press, 1949.

IAN JACK *Augustan Satire; Intention and Idiom in English Poetry 1660–1750.* Clarendon Press, 1952.

J. B. LEISHMAN *The Monarch of Wit; An Analytical and Comparative Study of the Poetry of John Donne.* Hutchinson & Co., 5th ed., 1962.

H. E. TOLIVER *Marvell's Ironic Vision.* Yale University Press, 1965.

R. M. ALDEN *The Rise of Formal Satire in England under Classical Influence.* Archon Books, 1961.

R. C. ELLIOTT *The Power of Satire; Magic, Ritual, Art.* Princeton University Press, 1960.

ALVIN KERNAN *The Cankered Muse, Satire of the English Renaissance.* Yale University Press, 1959.

JOHN PETER *Complaint and Satire in Early English Literature.* Clarendon Press, 1956.

HUGH WALKER *English Satire and Satirists.* J. M. Dent & Sons, 1925.

JAMES SUTHERLAND *English Satire.* Cambridge University Press, 1958.

RONALD PAULSON *The Fictions of Satire.* Johns Hopkins Press, 1967.

DAVID WORCESTER *The Art of Satire.* Harvard University Press, 1940.

Chronological List of Authors and Poems Quoted

HORACE (65–8 B.C.)
 from *Book* I, *Satire* I (translated by John Conington).
OVID (43 B.C.–A.D. 18)
 from *Ibis* (translated by Thomas Underdowne).
SENECA (d. A.D. 65)
 from the *Apocolocyntosis* (translated by Robert Graves).
PERSIUS (A.D. 34–62)
 from the *Second Satire* (translated by William Gifford).
JUVENAL (*c.* A.D. 60–130)
 from *The Sixth Satire* (translated by Dryden).
ALEXANDER BARCLAY (1475?–1552)
 from *The Ship of Fools*
 from *Of Inprofytable Bokes*
 from *Of New Fassions and Disgised Garmentes.*
JOHN SKELTON (1460?–1529)
 from *The Bouge of Court*
 from *Speak Parrot*
 from *Colin Clout*
 from *Why Come Ye not to Court?*
SIR THOMAS WYATT (1503?–42)
 from the *First Satire*
 from the *Second Satire.*
GEORGE GASCOIGNE (1515?–77)
 from *The Steele Glas.*
EDMUND SPENSER (1552?–99)
 from *Mother Hubbard's Tale.*
JOHN DONNE (1572–1631)
 from *Satire I*
 from *Satire IV*
 from *Satire VI*
 from *Satire III.*
JOHN MARSTON (1575?–1634)
 from *The Scourge of Villainie*
  Liber Primus Proemium

from *English Bards and Scotch Reviewers*
from *Don Juan Canto I*
from *The Vision of Judgement.*

PERCY BYSSHE SHELLEY (1792–1822)
from *Letter to Maria Gisborne*
from *Peter Bell the Third*
from *The Masque of Anarchy.*

JOHN KEATS (1795–1821)
from *The Cap and Bells.*

WINTHROP MACKWORTH PRAED (1802–39)
from *The New Order of Things*
from *Goodnight to the Season.*

EDWARD BULWER-LYTTON (1803–73)
from *The New Timon.*

ALFRED, LORD TENNYSON (1809–92)
from *The New Timon and the Poets.*

ROBERT BROWNING (1812–89)
To Edward FitzGerald.

COVENTRY PATMORE (1823–96)
from *1867.*

ARTHUR HUGH CLOUGH (1819–61)
from *Amours de Voyage*
The Latest Decalogue.

ALFRED AUSTIN (1835–1913)
from *The Season.*

T. S. ELIOT (1888–1965)
from *The Hippopotamus.*

JAMES JOYCE (1882–1941)
from *The Holy Office.*

WYNDHAM LEWIS (1884–1957)
from *One-way Song.*

ROY CAMPBELL (1902–57)
from *The Wayzgoose*
from *The Georgiad.*

W. H. AUDEN (b. 1907)
from *Letter to Lord Byron.*

JULIAN BELL (1908–37)
from *An Epistle on the Subject of the Ethical and Aesthetic Beliefs of Herr Ludwig Wittgenstein.*

HUGH MACDIARMID (b. 1892)
from *Your Immortal Memory, Burns.*